Why Can't I Get It Together? (ADHD Edition)

Executive Function for Adults With ADHD

Patty R. Adams

Table of Contents

Track Your Progress, One Week at a Time

Want to see how your executive function skills are evolving?

Scan the QR code below to access the free **Executive Function Snapshot Tracker** — a simple, weekly tool to help you reflect, reset, and notice what's working.

- Rate your focus, memory, time management, and more

- Set small goals and build self-awareness without shame

- Use it digitally or print it out and add it to your journal

Start where you are. Track as you go. Celebrate every win.

Just scan and get started!

Introduction

Life is tough for most people; however, for some, it's challenging to navigate even the basics of living. What's worse is many people have no idea why they're struggling so much to do the things others have no difficulty carrying out.

For people with attention deficit hyperactivity disorder (ADHD), forgetting where they put their car keys or wallet is commonplace, and they also have to deal with procrastination, impulsivity, lack of motivation, failed relationships, and more. That's a lot! No wonder they often feel like their life is spiraling out of control.

The fact that you're reading this book means you've been diagnosed with, or you suspect you have, ADHD. You're probably frustrated and are desperately looking for a way to get it together. I'm here to help.

I wish someone would've told *me* how to manage my ADHD. I would not have missed out on so many opportunities due to my disorganized mind. I was alone in navigating a life that felt totally off the rails for a long time. At first, I had no idea I had ADHD, and it wasn't until I went for professional help that I was diagnosed. Identifying what was "wrong" with me changed my life. The ability to put a name to it meant I could learn how to deal with all these quirks that prevented me from excelling in life.

Now, here I am. It's my mission to assist others in learning how to live with ADHD and not be prisoners of their minds. After reading this book, you'll have the skills to not only plan for the future you want but to also successfully execute your plan to reach your goal. We will work on executive functions specifically, including improving your attention and focus, increasing your memory, working on time management, and beating procrastination. With these skills, you'll be able to stay focused on your goals while having the self-control to overcome the symptoms that want to derail you.

These executive functions originate in the brain's prefrontal cortex, making it the CEO of your mind. Your prefrontal cortex has to manage many tasks, much like the head of a big organization. When you have ADHD, the CEO of your mind is a little lazy, and they're not very good at regulating focus and attention, fail at controlling impulses, can't remember information, and struggle to plan and organize. Compared to neurotypical individuals, those with ADHD have structural and functional differences in the prefrontal cortex (Hoogman et al., 2019). This means you'll have to learn to adapt to a world that wasn't created for those of us who function differently.

We also need to look at the role of specific neurotransmitters. Dopamine and norepinephrine play essential roles in helping us focus. These neurotransmitters are involved in regulating attention, motivation, and reward processing. Dopamine is often referred to as the "feel-good" neurotransmitter, and it is linked to feelings of pleasure and satisfaction. On the other hand, norepinephrine acts as both a neurotransmitter and a hormone, playing a crucial role in the body's fight-or-flight response.

In individuals without ADHD, dopamine and norepinephrine work together to help maintain focus and attention. Dopamine promotes feelings of reward and reinforcement, while norepinephrine helps regulate alertness and concentration. However, if you have ADHD, there is often dysregulation in the levels and functioning of these neurotransmitters, leading to difficulties in sustaining attention and staying focused. This imbalance may result in symptoms such as impulsivity, hyperactivity, and distractibility, which can impact daily functioning and cognitive performance.

If you're unsure if you have ADHD, here's an executive functioning self-assessment you can do that may give you a clearer indication. Keep in mind that this test is for informational purposes only and shouldn't be used to diagnose anyone. For a formal diagnosis, it is best to see a professional.

Quick ADHD Self-Assessment

Complete the following checklist to better understand your prefrontal cortex and your ability to function normally. Please know that when I say "normally," I'm talking about what society deems "normal." For many, ADHD is as normal as it gets, as it's the only way of existence they know. As they say, what's normal for the spider spells disaster for the fly, so it's all relative in the end.

Okay, time to answer some questions honestly to see what's what:

Do you remember what you learn and can recall facts on

important subjects?

Are you structured and organized in your work life?

Do you have control over your feelings and don't act out impulsively?

Do you execute tasks as planned?

Do you question yourself when making important decisions?

Do you have the ability to prioritize what tasks need to be done first?

Can you meet deadlines?

Are you flexible enough to adapt to change?

Have you set a goal and given up everything else to achieve this goal?

Can you work under pressure?

Do you understand how one thing relates to another? For example, shapes, letters, and words.

Do you enjoy solving mathematical problems?

Can you communicate clearly and quickly without losing the crux of the message?

Do you pay full attention to certain things while getting bored or easily distracted by others?

Can you pay attention to the small details when busy with challenging activities?

Can you link different information types and organize them into specific categories?

Do you think things through before making decisions or taking action?

The more "yes" answers you have, the higher the possibility that you have ADHD and should see a doctor for a professional diagnosis.

Whether you have been diagnosed by a doctor or only suspect you may have ADHD, the day you open this book marks the beginning of a journey to discover the incredible power within you, empowering you to manage your symptoms and transform your life. Welcome to a world of endless possibilities and newfound strengths waiting to be embraced. I think it's time we get going, don't you?

Chapter 1:

Attention and Focus

For anyone to achieve personal and professional success, they need to be able to pay attention and focus on the things that are important. These two factors are integral in how well you do something and how fast you complete tasks. Considering that the world has become so fast-paced, it's more important now than before to understand how to improve your attention and enhance your focus effectively. Distractions are everywhere, so you need to master these skills to boost your productivity and, so doing, reduce stress.

This chapter will look at various techniques and habits that will help you improve attention and sharpen your focus. We'll look at how hyperfocus—a characteristic of ADHD—can be both a blessing and a curse. We'll also explore how mindfulness practices can cultivate better concentration and how simple tools like timers can make a difference in staying focused.

By the end of this chapter, you'll have a better grasp of the strategies you need to apply to keep your mind on track and manage distractions, leading you to accomplish your goals more efficiently.

Understanding Focus and Attention in People With ADHD

People don't grasp the unique challenges those with ADHD face when it comes to focus and attention. It's often a constant struggle to maintain concentration, which can be extremely frustrating and result in decreased productivity. It's like trying to keep a tight grip on a slippery bar of soap, but just when you think you've got it, it slips away. We don't just face momentary lapses in attention but have to fight against distractions, both external and internal, making everyday activities significantly harder.

Let's delve deeper into what focus is so we can understand where we fall short (or excel).

More on Focus

Focus can be understood as the ability to direct your mental effort toward a specific thought or task. I like to think of it as having a spotlight in my mind that highlights what I'm concentrating on while blacking everything else out. This is an active process that requires conscious effort to maintain, and for those with ADHD, the spotlight will flicker or dim every now and again, making it harder to stay on task.

When a neurotypical person is listening to a podcast while driving in traffic, they have the ability to tune out the noise from other cars and even their own thoughts to focus on what is being said. For those of us with ADHD, this type of selective concentration is particularly challenging because external stimuli can easily pull our attention away. Without focus, it's impossible to finish any task you've started. Lacking focus often leads to a constant feeling of playing catch-up, which can be extremely tiring.

In the introduction, I talked about the CEO of your brain—the prefrontal cortex. When it comes to focus, this area acts like a control tower, directing your attention and ensuring you stick to what you're doing. For neurodivergent people, the control tower is less effective, which leads to difficulties in concentrating.

With a clearer understanding of focus, you're better able to acknowledge its importance and the challenges those with ADHD face in maintaining it. When you recognize that focus isn't just a matter of willpower but a process deeply tied to complex brain functions, you can start to work on strategies to help you cope with the challenges you may face. Understanding the brain's role in focus helps to demystify why specific strategies and treatments are effective for those with ADHD. Understanding this, you can approach treatment with greater clarity and purpose.

Why Is Focus Difficult for People With ADHD?

We've established that ADHD affects the brain's executive functions that help you pay attention, focus, and organize. When these functions are impaired, it becomes exceedingly difficult to perform everyday tasks efficiently, which can quickly lead to a chaotic lifestyle.

One of the hallmarks of ADHD is an overactive mind—something that contributes to difficulties maintaining focus. I don't know about you, but I have a near-constant stream of thoughts running through my mind, making it hard for me to pay attention to one thing for an extended period. I find this internal distraction to be not only exhausting but also overwhelming, and I've often said it is a primary cause of stress and anxiety in my life. It's like having several tabs open on the computer at once, and I just can't figure out which one to focus on first.

Coupled with this, there's the issue of external stimuli. For many with ADHD, the sound of a ticking clock, conversations in the next room, or even visual distractions can become overwhelming. This heightened sensitivity means that any task that requires sustained attention may seem insurmountable as your brain constantly shifts its focus.

Then there's impulsivity—another significant characteristic of ADHD that affects focus. Imagine starting an important report, but halfway through, you remember you need to send a pressing mail. While drafting the mail, you need to look something up online, but before you know it, you're checking social media instead. This constant shifting impedes your productivity and creates a sense of unfinished business, adding to the overall stress and frustration.

But impulsivity isn't just limited to task-switching; it also affects a person's decision-making processes. I have many unfished products lying around because I always impulsively decide to start a new project before completing the current one. This behavior further compounds difficulties in focusing as there's always something new and exciting pulling your attention away from what you should be doing.

Beyond these challenges, the cumulative effect of ADHD on life in general can be profound. Our inability to self-regulate our overactive minds, sensory load, and our impulsivity create a perfect storm that makes concentrating on even the simplest of tasks challenging. All these factors interact in complex ways, exacerbating each other and leading to a cycle of distraction and frustration. Misplacing items, forgetting appointments, and struggling to follow conversations are only some of the consequences of ADHD. No wonder people with ADHD often describe their lives as a constant battle to stay ahead of these symptoms while feeling perpetually behind.

The intricacy of ADHD emphasizes the importance of treating yourself with compassion. It's not merely about lacking willpower; it's a fundamental difference in how your brain operates. Acknowledging this is the first step to self-love and working toward strategies that can help mitigate the challenges you face in a healthy way.

While discussing these points, remember that everyone's experience with ADHD is unique. You may not experience it exactly the same as I have or as someone else with this brain disorder. This underscores why personalized approaches and flexibility are key to managing the condition effectively. Be persistent in finding what helps you, but be patient with yourself as you tackle the challenges associated with ADHD.

Hyperfocus: A Double-Edged Sword

Heightened focus is a fascinating phenomenon that plays a vital role in a person's productivity and creativity, especially for those with ADHD. Hyperfocus can be described as becoming fully immersed in a task with intense concentration. This state can lead to remarkable levels of productivity and out-of-the-box thinking. That's because it allows you to channel all your mental energy into one activity. Often, people get so immersed in what they're doing that they don't realize how much time has passed.

A key advantage of hyperfocus is its ability to enable "deep work" that involves concentrating on mentally demanding tasks for a long time without distraction. Not something someone with ADHD can do easily, right? However, when you do enter a hyperfocused state, you may experience what is called a "flow state"—where your sense of time vanishes, and you find yourself completely absorbed in what you're doing. This total immersion allows for breakthroughs in problem-solving and enhances creative output. Do you see why hyperfocus is incredibly valuable for those with ADHD?

But hyperfocus isn't all fun and games. It can happen that while you're in such a focused state, you neglect other important responsibilities. I got so fixated on a project once that the dishes and washing piled up, and I didn't even take care of my basic needs like eating and sleeping. What's worse, I was obsessing over trivial tasks that didn't contribute significant value to what I was doing, leading to wasted time and effort. I had to learn how to harness and control hyperfocus for it to stop being a liability and instead become a powerful asset.

It's crucial to strike a balance to avoid the pitfalls associated with hyperfocus. By setting clear boundaries and using tools like timers and reminders, you can ensure that you remain aware of your other obligations while still benefiting from the deep concentration hyperfocus offers. It all begins with recognizing the triggers and cues. For example, if you know that you tend to lose track of time while gardening, you should take extra measures to "pull you out" of the hyperfocused state—setting an alarm on your phone for when you want your time in the garden to be up as one way to bring you back to reality.

I also suggest you incorporate mindfulness practices into your daily life to develop an awareness of when hyperfocus occurs. This will allow for better management and control over this state.

One thing is certain: Harnessing hyperfocus can be a game-changer if you're striving to improve your productivity and achieve more in life. I think of it as a superpower, and I'm grateful that it is a common trait in individuals with ADHD. After learning to understand and control my hyperfocus, I've seen an amazing improvement in my time-management skills, as well as my productivity.

I do have to mention that people tend to use "hyperfocus" and "hyperfixation" interchangeably when they're not the same thing. Think of hyperfocus as the good guy and hyperfixation as its bad-boy cousin. Hyperfixation is exactly what you don't want to do; that is, become fixated on an activity that leads to negative consequences like ignoring your basic needs.

Scenario: Jenny was passionate about graphic design and decided to take on a personal project to create a digital illustration for a local art competition. As she immersed herself in the creative process, Jenny experienced a state of hyperfocus, where she devoted hours to refining every detail of her artwork.

This hyperfocus soon became hyperfixation, during which Jenny neglected other significant responsibilities, such as studying for upcoming exams, attending classes, and managing her daily chores. Despite reminders and approaching deadlines, Jenny found it difficult to shift her attention away from the artwork that captivated her.

As days passed, Jenny's hyperfixation on the art project intensified, leading her to spend late nights working on the illustration while neglecting essential self-care activities such as proper meals, adequate sleep, and exercise. The all-consuming nature of her hyperfixation gradually isolated Jenny from her usual routines and obligations.

As a result of her fixation on the art project, Jenny missed important deadlines for academic assignments, neglected social engagements with friends, and experienced increased stress and anxiety due to the mounting pressure of unmet responsibilities. The intense focus on the artwork created a tunnel vision effect, narrowing Jenny's attention solely to the creative task at hand to the detriment of other aspects of her life.

Realizing the negative impact of her hyperfocus on neglecting essential responsibilities, Jenny sought support from a counselor specializing in ADHD. Through guidance, she learned strategies to balance her intense interests with daily responsibilities, set boundaries on hyperfixation periods, and prioritize tasks effectively to prevent neglect of essential duties in the future.

By recognizing the challenges of hyperfixation and developing coping mechanisms to manage her intense focus, Jenny aimed to create a more balanced approach to her passions while honoring her commitments, maintaining well-being, and fostering a sense of harmony in her academic and personal life.

To prevent hyperfocus from turning into hyperfixation, it's essential to set boundaries and use time management techniques. Allow yourself breaks and prioritize tasks effectively.

So, as you move forward, think about how you can stop hyperfocus from changing into hyperfixation. If you feel your focus shifting too intensely, try redirecting your attention to other activities or seeking professional guidance if needed. Find strategies you can implement to make sure this stage enhances your progress and doesn't hinder it. Just remind yourself that the journey to mastering your attention and focus is ongoing, and using hyperfocus to your advantage brings you a step closer to finding the balance and success you're aiming for.

Strategies to Improve Focus

ADHD makes maintaining focus feel like an uphill battle; however, establishing a structured routine can minimize distractions and enhance predictability. For example, waking up and going to bed at the same time daily adds a consistent rhythm to your day. This helps ease the overwhelming feeling of chaos that often goes hand in hand with ADHD.

Also, I found that breaking your day into smaller, manageable blocks of time also helps. Instead of having a list of tasks that seem insurmountable, you should allocate specific times for each activity. I designate morning hours for writing or studying, afternoons for physical activities and exercise, and evenings for relaxing endeavors. I can't emphasize enough how this structure reduced my anxiety and improved productivity—I know precisely what I should be doing at any given moment.

That being said, it's essential to keep this routine flexible. Life happens, making strict adherence to a schedule near impossible. Build some buffer time into your routine to accommodate unexpected events. This flexibility ensures that your routine helps you and doesn't add to your stress. A flexible mindset will also help maintain a balance between staying on task and managing spontaneous events. This makes any routine sustainable over the long term.

Let's look at some more tools you can use to improve your focus:

Planners and Timers

These tools can make a huge difference in prioritizing tasks and managing time effectively. Planners are great for jotting down everything from tiny tasks to important appointments. When you see everything laid out visually, it will be easier to prioritize what needs your immediate attention versus what can wait. I like to think of my daily planner as a memory aid that reduces the cognitive load that often overwhelms me.

Timers are equally useful. The Pomodoro technique is an excellent example of a time management method that helps you make the most of your time. This technique involves working for 25 minutes and then taking a short break (The Pomodoro Technique, n.d.). This method uses timers to create a sense of urgency, and this helps maintain focus for a short burst of time; the breaks, in turn, prevent burnout. In time, timers like these can train your break to understand that concentrated effort is followed by relaxation, which makes it easier to stick to your tasks.

Breaks and Physical Activity

Building on the previous point, taking regular breaks can do wonders for refreshing the mind and sustaining attention throughout the day. Adding physical activity during your breaks amplifies the benefits. Strenuous exercise is not necessary; simply standing up, stretching, or walking around can refresh your mind and body.

Physical activity has been linked with improved focus and cognitive function (Mandolesi et al., 2018). Exercise releases "happy hormones" like dopamine, which helps enhance mood and attention. For this reason, I highly recommend you integrate movement into your daily routine in creative ways to keep you motivated to stay physically active. Working from home, I always take phone calls standing up, which allows me to pace around the room. This minor adjustment really adds up and allows me to stay active even when my schedule doesn't allow for time to exercise. It's good to know that short bursts of activity are just as beneficial as longer exercise sessions, making it easier to fit more naturally into your day.

Apps

We're fortunate to have digital tools as an extra layer of support. There are numerous apps designed for task management that can help you keep track of projects and deadlines. Whatever you need help with, there's bound to be an app out there for you. Over time, using these tools becomes a habit, leaving you with a toolbox filled with the means to manage your daily responsibilities more effectively. Sometimes, setting a reminder or alarm is all you need to stop anything important from slipping through the cracks.

Mindfulness and Meditation

Being mindful can significantly increase your awareness and help you control your focus. Mindfulness involves paying attention to the present while holding back any judgment. This can help you become more aware of where your mind is drifting. Many mindfulness exercises, like focusing on your breath for a few minutes, can ground you during those times when distractions arise.

Meditation is a step up from mindfulness. Its focus is on training the brain to pay attention to a single point of concentration, such as breathing, saying a mantra, or visualizing something specific. With regular meditation, you build mental discipline, which makes it easier to bring your focus back when your mind strays.

What I appreciate about meditation is that it doesn't have to take up too much time of your day. Short daily meditation sessions can lead to significant change over time, helping to rewire the brain for better focus and emotional regulation. What's more, you don't need to reserve a set time for mindfulness or meditation unless you want to. For example, savoring each bite of food and tuning into the flavors and texture combinations are considered mindful eating. By trying to be more mindful during your everyday activities, you train your brain, and whatever you're doing will be more enriching as you'll be in the moment!

The Role of Medication and Therapy

When it comes to managing ADHD, there are various pharmacological interventions you can explore to enhance focus and concentration. Methylphenidate (Ritalin, Concerta, etc.) and amphetamines are commonly prescribed. These medications work by altering the balance of certain neurotransmitters in the brain, especially dopamine and norepinephrine.

It is essential to approach medication with a clear understanding of how it works and what potential side effects to look out for. Many people experience significant improvement in ADHD symptoms, but some individuals encounter challenges such as appetite suppression, sleep disturbances, and increased heart rate. This is why working closely with your healthcare provider is important to finding the right dosage and monitoring any adverse effects. Unfortunately, these medications aren't a one-size-fits-all solution, so what works for me may not work for you, and that is why many tweaks may be necessary.

You should also keep in mind that medication might not address all aspects of ADHD. It's true that it can enhance concentration and so on, but it can't teach you how to navigate the complexities of living with ADHD. This is where behavior therapy comes into play; it's a great complementary strategy to manage attention while helping you deal with life in general.

Therapy usually involves structured approaches to developing coping mechanisms and skills tailored to every individual's needs. Cognitive behavioral therapy (CBT), for example, helps you identify and modify negative thought patterns, enables you to regulate your emotions, and teaches you how to respond to distractions. CBT focuses on practical solutions to problems you may face. For example, your therapist tells you to restructure your thinking from "I can never stay focused" to "I can learn specific strategies to improve my focus." Over time, these positive changes in thinking will lead to reduced anxiety related to ADHD, and this is another step in improving your attention.

Therapists often help you establish routines and organizational systems that can minimize distractions. They use visual aids, set goals, and show you how to break these tasks into smaller, manageable steps. They may also introduce you to mindfulness techniques that will increase your awareness and control over your focus, reducing the impact of ADHD symptoms in daily life.

Ultimately, integrating medication and therapy requires careful coordination between you, your healthcare professional, and your therapist. You'll need to go for regular follow-ups and adjustments to ensure both components of your treatment plan are working well together. I can't stress enough how important it is for you to maintain open communication with your healthcare team and to express any concerns or changes you may have as soon as possible.

Key Takeaways

In this chapter, we looked at the concept of focus and its importance. Now that you know what focus is and why it tends to "flicker" for individuals with ADHD, I hope you realize that staying on task isn't just about willpower but involves complex brain functions. This understanding should motivate you to be kinder with yourself.

As someone with ADHD, you experience a relentless barrage of things that distract you—not only do you have an overactive mind, but you also have to deal with the constant pull of external stimuli. This makes holding attention feel like a monumental challenge. Thankfully, there are many practical strategies that can help you tackle these challenges. Using planners and timers, taking breaks, exercising, and practicing mindfulness are only some of the ways you can help anchor a wandering mind.

Medication and therapy are further components in the management of ADHD. With medications balancing neurotransmitters and offering you immediate relief from symptoms, therapy gives you the long-term skills and coping mechanisms to make the best of your life.

As we wrap up this chapter, it's essential to acknowledge the unique nature of each individual's experience. What works for one person might not work for another, underscoring the need for empathy and ongoing support.

In the next chapter, we will look at memory challenges people with ADHD face and how it can manifest in everyday tasks. Of course, we'll look at various ways you can make your daily life run smoother.

Chapter 2:

Working Memory

Working memory, the brain's ability to hold and recall information for short periods, often presents difficulties for those with ADHD. These challenges can manifest in everyday tasks like following a conversation or remembering instructions. Recognizing these nuances helps in appreciating why certain activities might be more demanding and sets the stage for exploring strategies to mitigate these issues.

In this chapter, we'll dive into the specifics of working memory difficulties faced by individuals with ADHD. We'll explore the cognitive processes involved and how they differ from those without the condition. You'll discover practical strategies designed to improve memory functioning and make daily life smoother. We'll cover various approaches to enhance working memory, from organizational tips to mental exercises. By understanding these techniques, you can better manage the demands of daily tasks and reduce the stress associated with memory lapses.

Explaining Working Memory and ADHD

Working memory is a person's ability to retain, recall, and process information for a brief period. This process unfolds within the frontal cortex of the brain, facilitating the holding of information while, at the same time, applying it to a task or problem.

Individuals with a great working memory shine in activities that call for intellectual multitasking, like mental calculations and tasks that involve mental imagery, such as finding their way through unknown terrain. Reading, note-taking, planning, and navigating directions come easier if you have a working memory that, well, works!

Working memory also plays a crucial role in regulating emotions. How interesting, right? Studies indicate that individuals with stronger working memory exhibit lower reactivity to events and demonstrate better capabilities in evaluating emotional situations compared to those with weaker working memory (Kaiser et al., 2021). Emotionally significant information is converted into long-term memory through the mechanisms of working memory, which are intricately linked to emotions.

Simple tasks are initially processed in short-term memory, while more complex and demanding information is handled by working memory. Information marked as emotionally significance or particularly relevant is stored in the long-term memory. Consequently, when faced with situations requiring such information, our brains are wired to retrieve and apply it effortlessly.

The Difference Between Working Memory and Short-Term Memory

Many people use the terms "working memory" and "short-term memory" interchangeably, but they're more like twins—separate yet interconnected. In general, short-term memory represents the ability to temporarily activate long-term memories on a short-term basis. On the other hand, working memory empowers individuals to work with a "chunk" of that memory by focusing and processing it in a tailored manner, involving the temporary storage and manipulation of information in the mind. For example, if you have a sharp short-term memory, you'll be able to effortlessly recall and repeat a series of numbers in the same order learned. However, without a robust working memory, you might face challenges when asked to rearrange the sequence, like reciting it backward.

One key difference between short-term and working memory is the latter's necessity to filter out distractions and discard irrelevant data. This explains why individuals with ADHD, even with strong short-term memory, grapple with working memory issues.

Influence of ADHD on Working Memory

ADHD exerts a significant influence on executive functioning, as you read earlier. If you experience challenges in working memory or a shortfall in core executive functioning skills, you may display "executive dysfunction."

Here's a look at how ADHD influences working memory:

When you have ADHD, you will most likely struggle with attention regulation, and this will affect your ability to maintain focus and retain information in working memory. This difficulty in sustaining attention can lead to lapses in memory and make it difficult to complete tasks.

We know that ADHD is associated with executive function deficits, including working memory impairment. When you find it difficult to organize and process information in real time, this will disrupt your working memory, which will affect your ability to retain and manipulate information.

The fact that people with ADHD find it difficult to control their inhibitions can interfere with their ability to filter out distractions and prioritize relevant information meant for storage and retrieval. That can lead to difficulties in focusing and recalling important details.

Task-switching and flexible thinking—two essential components of working memory—don't come easily to those with ADHD. The challenges of transitioning between tasks and adapting to changing demands put a lot of strain on working memory resources.

ADHD can influence a person's processing speed, affecting the efficiency of translating, storing, and retrieving information in working memory. This slower processing speed can hinder the accuracy of cognitive tasks that use working memory to function.

The fact that we struggle with short-term memory retention and retrieval makes it difficult to pay attention and follow through on tasks.

By understanding the impact of ADHD on working memory and implementing strategies to support cognitive functioning, you can optimize your working memory capacity, enhance focus and task performance, and navigate cognitive tasks more effectively in academic, professional, and daily life settings.

Scenario: Mark worked in a fast-paced marketing agency where he was responsible for managing multiple projects simultaneously. Due to his ADHD-related working memory challenges, Mark often struggled to retain and retrieve information, follow through on tasks, and stay organized in his role.

Despite setting reminders and creating task lists, Mark frequently forgot important deadlines and key project details. His working memory limitations made it challenging to retain crucial information and prioritize tasks effectively, leading to missed deadlines and increased stress.

His working memory difficulties also affected his communication skills. During client meetings or team discussions, he would struggle to recall important points, contribute relevant ideas, or follow complex discussions. This impacted his ability to communicate effectively and collaborate with colleagues.

He would often find himself starting multiple tasks but struggling to complete them due to his working memory limitations. He would forget critical steps in the project workflow, lose track of ongoing tasks, and experience difficulty maintaining focus and momentum to finish assignments in a timely manner.

Processing information efficiently was a significant challenge for Mark. He would become overwhelmed when presented with a large amount of data or instructions, leading to confusion, frustration, and decreased ability to make sound decisions or solve problems effectively.

Due to his working memory struggles, managing time effectively was particularly challenging for Mark. He would underestimate the time needed to complete tasks, experience difficulty prioritizing activities, and often feel overwhelmed by the demands of his workload, resulting in inefficiencies and delays.

Ultimately, Mark's working memory deficits hindered his ability to organize and plan tasks systematically. He often misplaced important documents, overlooked critical details in project briefs, and experienced difficulty in creating and following through on structured plans, impacting his productivity and efficiency. The daily challenges caused by his working memory difficulties took a toll on Mark's self-esteem and confidence. He often felt frustrated, inadequate, and overwhelmed by his perceived shortcomings, affecting his motivation, job satisfaction, and overall well-being.

Recognizing the profound impact of his working memory challenges on his daily life, Mark sought support from a cognitive-behavioral therapist specializing in ADHD. Through personalized interventions, skill-building exercises, and cognitive strategies, Mark aimed to enhance his working memory function, improve his organizational skills, and develop coping mechanisms to navigate the demands of his job more effectively.

By addressing his working memory deficits and implementing tailored interventions, Mark aspired to overcome the obstacles posed by ADHD in his professional life, enhance his work performance, and cultivate a sense of empowerment, resilience, and success in managing his daily challenges.

Despite the potential occurrence of working memory issues in neurotypical individuals, research underscores a strong association between ADHD and compromised working memory (Mukherjee et al., 2021). Brain scans of children with ADHD consistently reveal reduced brain activation specific to working memory tasks compared to non-ADHD peers. Given that ADHD is a lifelong condition, deficits in working memory persist into adulthood.

Enhancing Working Memory

For years, I played brain games and tried various ways to improve my memory. Unfortunately, these methods don't work as well as we need them to. While these exercises may gradually advance your ability to complete specific tasks, such as finding patterns and workarounds, these gains will be limited to those specific activities.

As someone with ADHD, you need to accept the fact that it's not truly possible to improve your working memory in such a way that it will make a significant difference in all areas of your life (Al-Saad et al., 2021). You'll have to learn to cope with a poor memory; the alternative will only lead to frustration and shame. Just as a person with diabetes can't deny their reality and refuse to take their medicine, so too can't people with ADHD force themselves to function as if they have an efficient working memory.

I found that acknowledging I had a working memory deficit was the first step in moving on. It allowed me to learn new skills, build new habits, and work around the problem. I started to approach tasks differently than my neurotypical peers did but, in the end, achieved the same results.

This book is all about teaching you a wide variety of skills and tools to function as an adult with ADHD. The following strategies will help you sidestep the memory issues that form part of your condition. Of course, everyone is different, so you'll have to try them all out to find out what works for you.

Get Into a Routine

If you can turn a task into a habit, you've taken a lot of the thinking out of it. Have you ever arrived home after a long day at the office but don't remember the drive? That's because getting in the car, driving, and even the road you travel have become habits and now require less working memory to complete. Turning something into a habit takes perseverance and a lot of energy in the beginning. That is why you shouldn't get discouraged when you're struggling. Take it slow and be patient with yourself, but most importantly, don't attempt to turn everything into a habit all at once. Take it one step at a time.

Make Lists

Have you ever thought of something you *have* to do *now*, but before you know it, it's jumbled with all the other to-do items in your mind and the urgency is gone? To avoid this, you should get into the habit of immediately writing it down when you think about it. I also like to list the steps required to do a complicated task before I start so I can cross things off as I finish them. Creating a list frees up mental space, which means you'll be able to give whatever you're doing your full attention.

Use Technology

Use the calendar on your phone to set reminders. Alternatively, download apps you can use to create lists and sort tasks. There are various apps to choose from; you just need to figure out what features you like and if the app meets your needs.

Don't Use Technology

There are many reasons why technology may not be the way to go for some. It may be too much of a temptation to quickly check social media and fall down a rabbit hole of scrolling for hours. Or, maybe it's a case of task alarms getting lost in a flood of messages and emails. Whatever the reason, if using digital tools isn't for you, don't use them! There's nothing wrong with pen and paper. Whiteboards, journals, or something as simple as taping a note to your car mirror to remind you to stop for milk can make a world of difference in your day-to-day life.

Avoid Multitasking

Let's say you're busy with an important task and something else you need to do randomly pops into your mind. What do you do? As someone with ADHD, you'll probably want to act on it immediately. However, that's not the way to go; instead, write it down and do it later. When you switch tasks continuously, you're more likely to lose track of what you were doing or may end up doing it badly. Down below, we'll look at more reasons why multitasking isn't a way to be productive at all.

Stay in the Moment

Our minds often drift to the past or future, and this can be very distracting. It can lead to shame, fear, and anxiety, opening yourself up to negative emotions that will make it harder for you to concentrate on what you're doing. Mindfulness practice can help you stay in the moment. Techniques like body scanning, breathwork, and visualization can help keep you focused on the present.

Multitasking vs. Monotasking

For individuals with ADHD, distinguishing between multitasking and monotasking is crucial to better understand how their cognitive processing styles align with these approaches.

Multitasking involves handling multiple tasks simultaneously or switching from one task to another rapidly. This can be particularly challenging due to difficulty maintaining sustained attention and focus. I'm sure I'm not the only person with ADHD who finds it difficult to cook dinner while answering emails and keeping an eye on my kids. While such chaos might seem like an everyday activity for others, it can be a significant hurdle for those with ADHD. Frequent distractions and shifting attention can result in incomplete tasks and increased stress.

People often think multitasking leads to greater productivity, but research suggests otherwise. Every switch between tasks requires the brain to reorient itself, and this leads to delays and even potential errors (Madore & Wagner, 2019). This is known as "tasking-switching cost," and the price is higher to pay if you have ADHD. For us, what seems like multitasking can quickly turn into a series of half-completed tasks, which leads to frustration and decreased productivity.

Conversely, monotasking focuses on completing one task at a time before moving on to the next. This is a much better approach for those with ADHD, considering our cognitive characteristics. Monotasking reduces cognitive load, which means our brains are dedicated to one particular activity. This focused attention is precisely what we need since we struggle with working memory. For example, following a detailed recipe step-by-step without trying to watch TV, engaging in conversation, or solving a problem will lead to a more satisfying (and successful) baking experience since your brain will be able to process the information more effectively.

Of course, it doesn't hurt that monotasking is known to improve the quality of work. When your attention isn't divided, you can produce higher-quality outcomes—it doesn't matter what you're doing. Monotasking is so effective—even for neurotypical people—that I taught my kids to dedicate an uninterrupted block of time to studying rather than fleeting moments of studying mixed in with other activities. I wasn't surprised when I saw their grades climbing because how they were studying now meant better comprehension and retention of information. When you apply this principle to other activities, you'll enhance both your productivity and self-esteem, as it provides tangible results that positively reinforce your effort.

Understanding these differences has profound practical implications. Once individuals recognize that monotasking leverages their cognitive strengths, they can create structured environments that support this approach. This could involve setting up specific times dedicated to individual tasks, using tools like planners and timers to stay on track, or creating physical spaces free of distracting elements. Such strategies not only accommodate the unique cognitive profile of someone with ADHD but also foster a sense of accomplishment and progress.

Let's have a quick side-by-side comparison of multitasking and monotasking to recap the good and bad qualities:

Pros and Cons of Multitasking and Monotasking

Multitasking Pros	Multitasking Cons

- The appeal of multitasking lies in its potential to juggle various responsibilities. Some people with ADHD find that quick shifts between tasks provide the novelty and stimulation that their brains crave. This adaptability can be an asset in managing diverse workloads and responsibilities.

- Frequent task switching can increase one's susceptibility to errors. Each time we shift our attention from one task to another, there's a cognitive cost involved. This "switching cost" means it takes time for our brain to reorient itself to the new task, leading to mistakes and decreased accuracy.

- Furthermore, the notion of increased productivity through multitasking may be misleading. Research indicates that the human brain isn't truly capable of handling multiple tasks at the same time. Instead, what we perceive as multitasking is actually just rapid task-switching, which fragments our attention.

- Another significant downside to multitasking is

the stress and cognitive overload it can generate. Managing several tasks at once demands constant mental juggling, which can quickly become exhausting.

Monotasking Pros	Monotasking Cons
• When someone with ADHD commits to monotasking, they often find that their ability to concentrate improves significantly. This is because fewer distractions are pulling their attention in different directions. By creating a more focused environment, the person can give their full attention to the task at hand. This increased concentration helps complete tasks more efficiently and allows the individual to dive deeper	• One potential downside is that it can result in slower progress when multiple tasks need attention. For some individuals with ADHD, this might lead to feelings of frustration or stress, especially if they feel like they're falling behind on other important tasks. • Strict adherence to monotasking can sometimes be at odds with the fast-paced demands of modern life. Many situations require multitasking, or at least the ability to shift focus swiftly

into the details of the task.

- Monotasking often leads to higher rates of task completion. People with ADHD sometimes struggle to finish what they start because other stimuli easily sidetrack their brains. By committing to one task at a time, they can build momentum and follow through until it is done. This sense of accomplishment can also boost self-esteem and reduce the frustration that comes from leaving multiple tasks incomplete.

- Another key advantage of monotasking is its impact on the quality of work produced. When someone with ADHD focuses on a single task, the likelihood of making mistakes diminishes.

from one task to another. People with ADHD might find it challenging to maintain a strict monotasking regimen when their environment doesn't support it. Flexibility and occasional adjustments in strategy are necessary to ensure that monotasking remains beneficial rather than becoming a source of additional stress.

Attention regulation, which is often challenging for those with ADHD, becomes more manageable in a monotasking environment.

- By reducing mistakes, individuals with ADHD can experience less anxiety related to their performance. Anxiety about making errors can be a significant barrier to productivity and learning. When tasks are handled one at a time with full focus, the individual's confidence in their abilities grows, promoting a more positive outlook on their capabilities. Over time, this can lead to a more proactive approach to taking on new challenges.

Key Takeaways

In this chapter, we examined working memory and ADHD. While you may not want to hear that you can't improve your working memory significantly, by implementing strategies such as making lists, sticking to routines, using technology, and staying in the moment, you can lead a more manageable and fulfilling life.

We also looked at how multitasking may not be the way to go if you have ADHD. Although it's widely believed that multitasking leads to greater productivity, it's not always the case. Switching between tasks means your brain needs to reorient itself, which takes time and can lead to potential errors. The last thing you want is to sit with half-completed tasks and not know where to begin to finish them all. Instead, you should focus on completing one task at a time.

Monotasking is a better approach if you have ADHD since it reduces cognitive load, making it easier for you to focus on completing the task and doing it well.

Implementing the strategies we covered in this chapter can help you feel less overwhelmed by daily tasks and more confident that you won't forget them! That's the power of understanding and applying these techniques.

In the next chapter, we will look at overcoming the anxiety that accompanies starting a task. I know that the mere thought of beginning a new project, no matter how small, can feel overwhelming because you can't help but think about your distractibility, impulsivity, and, ultimately, fear of failing. Taking the first step can seem impossible, which leads to procrastination and unfinished tasks. But don't worry; after reading the next chapter, you'll have all the practical tools you need to start tasks more efficiently and move forward easily!

Chapter 3:

Task Initiative

People with ADHD often struggle with starting tasks due to a combination of factors. For one, the fact that we're so easily distracted often leads to a fear of not finishing what we started and failing. Our impulsivity doesn't make matters any easier, as well.

In this chapter, we'll explore strategies to improve task initiation skills. You'll learn about breaking down larger tasks into manageable steps, setting realistic goals, and creating a supportive environment to encourage progress. We'll also dive into understanding the role of perfectionism in task initiation and how self-compassion can make a significant difference. By the end of this chapter, you'll have practical tools and insights to help you start tasks more easily and keep moving forward despite the challenges ADHD presents.

The Trap of Perfectionism

Perfectionism can be particularly challenging for individuals with ADHD. It often starts with setting unrealistically high standards for oneself; instead of aiming for progress, which is achievable, the focus shifts to an unattainable ideal. This mindset sets you up for disappointment and frustration should you fall short of these lofty goals. You may find these high standards paralyzing because the thought of not meeting them is overwhelming. That's why it's essential to understand that aiming for perfection can create significant barriers to even starting a task.

Shying Away From Perfectionism: Embracing Realism

Perfectionism can be detrimental to your well-being and can cause stress, anxiety, and a constant fear of failure. It's important to shift toward a more realistic approach to avoid the pitfalls of perfectionism.

Why Perfectionism Is Bad for You

- **Increased stress levels:** Constantly chasing perfection can elevate stress levels and affect your mental health.

- **Risk of procrastination:** The fear of not achieving perfection may lead to procrastination or avoidance of tasks.

- **Negative self-image:** Unrealistic standards can contribute to a negative self-image and reduce self-confidence.

- **Impaired relationships:** Striving for perfection can strain relationships due to high expectations from yourself and others.

Embracing Realism Tips

By adopting a more realistic mindset and embracing imperfections, you can alleviate the pressure of perfectionism and experience greater fulfillment and growth in your endeavors.

Start by setting realistic goals. Define achievable and specific goals that still challenge you but are within your reach. Working toward your goals, you should be kind to yourself. Acknowledge that making mistakes is a natural part of growth. In fact, don't see it as a failure at all; instead, see it as an opportunity to learn and improve.

Celebrating small victories is a great way to keep your mind from fixating on achieving perfection. Focus on your progress and acknowledge milestones along the way. You'll be too busy applauding yourself to have time to think about what you could've done better. Of course, don't get caught up in your success too much. Ask for feedback! The secret, however, is to stop yourself from seeing it as a measure of your worth.

Ultimately, you need to understand that perfection is unattainable. Train yourself to appreciate the beauty of imperfection.

I know that when perfectionism takes hold, the fear of making mistakes becomes a significant obstacle. The idea of doing something "less than perfect" leads me to delay starting tasks. This hesitation stems from a worry that any mistake will reflect poorly on my abilities. This fear can cause a cycle of inaction, where tasks are left unstarted and incomplete due to an unwillingness to risk errors. Recognizing this as a common pitfall was the first step towards mitigating its effects.

To move past this fear, it's crucial for you to embrace the concept that mistakes are a natural part of the learning process. Everyone makes mistakes, and each one provides a valuable opportunity to learn and grow. By shifting the perspective to see errors as stepping stones rather than setbacks, the pressure to be faultless diminishes. This understanding helps create a more forgiving environment, where taking action and making progress become more important than achieving perfection.

Scenario: Emily excelled academically throughout her school years, driven by her desire for perfection and high standards. However, her perfectionistic tendencies began to take a toll on her mental health and well-being as she entered the workforce and navigated adult responsibilities.

In college, Emily's quest for perfectionism intensified as she pursued top grades in all her courses. She spent excessive hours meticulously editing every assignment, seeking flawless outcomes, and struggling to delegate tasks or seek assistance when needed. This perfectionistic mindset created immense academic pressure and anxiety that impacted her overall performance and mental health.

Upon entering the workforce, Emily's perfectionism extended to her professional endeavors. She set unrealistic expectations for herself, aiming for flawless work output and perfection in every project she undertook. This relentless pursuit of perfection led to heightened stress, burnout, and difficulty meeting deadlines due to her meticulous attention to detail and fear of making mistakes.

Her perfectionistic tendencies influenced her interpersonal relationships negatively. She held herself and others to impossibly high standards, leading to frustration, conflict, and dissatisfaction in her interactions with colleagues, friends, and family members. The pressure she placed on herself to meet perfectionistic ideals strained her relationships and created communication barriers.

The constant pursuit of perfectionism fueled self-criticism and feelings of inadequacy in Emily. Despite external achievements, she struggled with imposter syndrome, comparing herself to unrealistic standards and internalizing a sense of failure whenever she fell short of perfection. This negative self-talk eroded her self-worth and self-esteem over time.

Emily's quest for perfectionism took a toll on her physical and mental health. The chronic stress, anxiety, and self-imposed pressure to excel in all areas of her life resulted in sleep disturbances, emotional exhaustion, and compromised well-being. The relentless pursuit of perfectionism affected her ability to prioritize self-care and maintain a healthy work-life balance.

Her perfectionistic mindset instilled a fear of failure and risk aversion in her decision-making process. She hesitated to take on new challenges, explore creative opportunities, or step outside her comfort zone due to the fear of making mistakes or falling short of perfection. This fear of failure hindered personal growth and inhibited her potential for innovation and resilience.

Recognizing the detrimental impact of her perfectionistic tendencies on her life, Emily sought support from a therapist. Through cognitive-behavioral therapy, mindfulness practices, and self-compassion exercises, Emily aimed to challenge her perfectionistic beliefs, embrace imperfection, and cultivate a healthier relationship with achievement, self-worth, and personal fulfillment.

By addressing the destructive effects of perfectionism in ADHD and fostering a sense of self-acceptance, resilience, and balance, Emily embarked on a journey of self-discovery, growth, and empowerment to reclaim control of her life and well-being.

Be Kind to Yourself

Developing self-compassion practices can also play a vital role in overcoming the paralyzing effects of perfectionism. Self-compassion involves treating oneself with kindness and understanding, especially in the face of failure or difficulty. You need to give yourself permission to be imperfect because you're only human, and we're all flawed. In practical terms, it means permitting yourself to be imperfect and recognizing that imperfection is a shared human experience. This approach can significantly reduce the self-imposed pressure to perform flawlessly.

Engaging in self-compassionate thinking can make a notable difference in how you approach tasks. For instance, instead of harshly criticizing yourself for procrastinating due to perfectionist tendencies, it helps to acknowledge your struggle and offer words of encouragement. Practicing phrases like "It's okay to start small" or "Everyone learns from their mistakes" can foster a more supportive internal dialogue. Over time, this constructive mindset reduces the anxiety associated with beginning new tasks.

Moreover, implementing small acts of self-kindness can solidify this practice. These acts might include rewarding oneself for completing parts of a task or taking breaks without guilt. Small gestures of self-care help reinforce the notion that one's worth is not contingent on perfect performance. This shift in attitude can lead to a more balanced approach to work and life in general.

Procrastination

Procrastination is a common struggle for individuals with ADHD, often stemming from feeling overwhelmed by tasks. This overwhelming sensation can paralyze you, making even the simplest task seem insurmountable. Many people with ADHD find that large projects or lengthy to-do lists trigger anxiety because they don't know where to start. The sheer magnitude of what needs to be accomplished can cloud your ability to take the first step.

You may procrastinate for various other reasons related to the core symptoms of the condition and associated challenges. Here are some factors that contribute to procrastination in individuals with ADHD:

- **Task initiation challenges:** Initiating tasks, especially those perceived as boring, monotonous, or overwhelming, can be particularly difficult. The initial energy required to start a task may be too high, causing delays and procrastination.

- **Impulsivity:** Impulsivity, a common trait in ADHD, can manifest as acting on immediate impulses or desires rather than engaging in planned or goal-directed behavior. Impulsive choices and decision-making can lead to procrastination by prioritizing short-term gratification over long-term goals.

- **Lack of structure or routine:** You may struggle to establish routines, maintain schedules, and create a structured environment conducive to productivity. This absence of a clear routine or organizational system can contribute to procrastination and delays in task completion.

- **Difficulty with prioritization:** Difficulty prioritizing tasks and determining the most important or urgent activities can result in procrastination. Without a clear sense of priorities, you may delay important tasks in favor of less critical or more immediately gratifying activities.

By understanding the underlying reasons for procrastination in ADHD and implementing strategies to address executive function deficits, improve time management skills, manage distractions, and establish effective routines, you can navigate procrastination more effectively and enhance your productivity and task completion.

Coping With Procrastination

Extensive projects or long to-do lists provoke anxiety in me because I find it difficult to determine where to begin. The vastness of the tasks at hand clouds my judgment, hindering me from taking the first step and just doing it!

To combat procrastination associated with ADHD, I learned that breaking down tasks into smaller, more manageable segments is beneficial. By dividing tasks into simpler components, I feel less overwhelmed and start to make progress gradually. Moreover, setting clear, achievable goals for each segment provides a sense of direction and accomplishment throughout the process.

I'm not the only person with ADHD who had to learn this the hard way. A friend of mine is a graphic designer. When I last saw her, she had a big project involving multiple stages: brainstorming, sketching, revisions, and finalizing designs. I remember her complaining that she felt overwhelmed with everything that needed to be done. Her anxiety kicked in, causing her to put off the project altogether. Since she also has ADHD, it was difficult for her to navigate through this haze of panic and disorganization.

A practical approach would be breaking down these massive tasks into smaller, more manageable steps. Focusing on one small part at a time makes the task less intimidating. For instance, instead of tackling the entire design project, Jane could start by brainstorming ideas and moving to sketches only when that initial stage is complete. This method reduces the sense of being overwhelmed and provides a clear path forward, making each step feel achievable. We'll talk about this in more depth later.

Here are some other techniques you can give a try to beat procrastination:

Work in a Structured Manner

Establishing a structured environment can help you overcome procrastination. Maintaining an organized workspace with necessary materials readily accessible can minimize distractions and enhance focus. Additionally, using tools such as calendars, planners, or task management apps can help you prioritize tasks and set realistic deadlines.

Implement Time Management Techniques

Effective time management techniques can significantly benefit anyone with ADHD in combating procrastination. Utilizing strategies like the Pomodoro Technique, which involves working in intervals with short breaks, can enhance productivity and prevent tasks from feeling overwhelming. Furthermore, scheduling specific times for tasks and setting timers for each activity can assist in maintaining focus and avoiding procrastination.

Seek Support and Accountability

Reaching out to friends, family, or support groups for help dealing with procrastination can leave you feeling encouraged. Moreover, it keeps you accountable. Engaging with a therapist or coach specialized in ADHD can offer valuable strategies and guidance tailored to individual needs. Moreover, sharing progress with a trusted individual and celebrating achievements, no matter how small, can boost motivation and deter procrastination tendencies.

Work on Something That Interests You

Another significant factor contributing to procrastination is a lack of motivation or interest in the task at hand. When I'm not genuinely interested in a task, I find it hard to muster the energy and focus required to begin. This is often because routine or mundane tasks fail to capture my attention. I find that pairing a tedious task with something enjoyable, like listening to music or working alongside a friend, can make it more appealing. Furthermore, setting specific goals and deadlines significantly boosts my motivation. That's because clearly defining what needs to be done and by when creates a sense of urgency.

Work Smart

Breaking tasks into smaller parts helps manage feeling overwhelmed and addresses the issue of maintaining sustained attention. Smaller tasks are easier to start and complete, providing frequent moments of accomplishment, which can be highly motivating. These small wins create a positive feedback loop, encouraging continued progress.

Using tools like checklists can offer additional support in breaking down tasks. By visualizing the smaller components of a larger project, you'll be able to track your progress more effectively. Checking items off a list provides a tangible reward, reinforcing the habit of gradually starting and finishing tasks. We discussed this in-depth in the previous chapter.

Set a Deadline and Stick to It!

Implementing specific deadlines and using timers can significantly improve focus and productivity. Deadlines create a framework within which tasks must be completed, reducing the likelihood of indefinite delays. Timers are a constant reminder of the passage of time, helping you stay on task and avoid distractions.

Deadlines and timers also introduce a competitive element, turning task completion into a game. I found this to be particularly effective for ADHD minds since we often respond well to challenges and immediate rewards. A playful approach transforms mundane tasks into exciting objectives, promoting better time management and task initiation.

Progress Over Time

Recognizing progress over time is crucial if you have ADHD. It can significantly enhance both motivation and a sense of achievement. One practical way to acknowledge this progress is by tracking it in a journal or an app designed for this purpose. When you look back at where you started, even the small steps forward become evident. This realization boosts your morale and encourages you to keep moving toward your goals.

Imagine setting out to read a book that seems overwhelming. Logging each chapter you complete provides a visual representation of your progress. This incremental tracking makes the entire task less daunting and more manageable. Each logged entry acts as a mini-celebration of your effort, creating a snowball effect that enhances your drive to continue.

The journey of a thousand miles begins with a single step, and documenting these steps allows you to see your journey unfold. Overcoming challenges, no matter how minor they may seem, builds resilience. The act of tracking serves as a constant reminder that you are advancing, which can be especially uplifting on days when progress feels slow.

Reviewing past successes is another powerful tool to boost confidence in completing future tasks. Successes, no matter how small, serve as proof that you have the capability to achieve what you set out to do. Think back to the last time you faced a challenging task and completed it successfully. Reflecting on this success can fortify your belief in your ability to tackle new challenges.

A simple yet effective method for reviewing past successes is keeping a "success log." Whenever you accomplish something, jot it down along with how it made you feel. On days when you doubt your abilities, reading through this log can remind you of your potential and previous triumphs. It is about recalling what was achieved and reconnecting with the positive emotions associated with those achievements.

Here's an example of a Success Log:

Date: Monday, July 22, 2024

Successes:

1. **Professional Success:**

   ○ Completed a challenging project ahead of the deadline.

   ○ Received positive feedback from the client for the quality of work.

2. **Personal Growth:**

   ○ Attended a virtual networking event and connected with industry professionals.

   ○ Started a new book on personal development and completed the first chapter.

3. **Health and Wellness:**

   ○ Went for a 30-minute morning jog to kickstart the day.

   ○ Prepared a nutritious meal for lunch and avoided unhealthy snacking.

Reflections:

Today was a productive day where I accomplished tasks both professionally and personally. I managed my time effectively and maintained a balance between work and self-care. The positive feedback I received boosted my confidence, and networking opportunities opened up new possibilities. Taking care of my physical health with exercise and healthy eating contributed to my overall well-being. Reflecting on these successes motivates me to strive for excellence and personal growth daily.

Confidence is built incrementally. It's like laying bricks; each successful task is another brick that strengthens the structure of your self-belief. By regularly reviewing your past successes, you're continually reinforcing that foundation, making it easier to take on more significant and complex tasks in the future.

Consider setting aside a few minutes at the end of each week to reflect on what went well and what could be improved. Write down your thoughts and consider any adjustments needed for the coming week. This practice consolidates your achievements and aligns your future efforts with what you've learned.

Positive reflection feeds into habit formation. When you recognize and appreciate your progress, it becomes easier to repeat the behaviors that led to that success. Over time, these repeated, intentional actions solidify into habits, making it almost second nature to initiate and complete tasks effectively.

Breaking Bigger Jobs Into Smaller Tasks

A large task can leave you feeling overwhelmed. My mother always asked me, "How do you eat an elephant?" I'd reply, "One bite at a time." This is a lesson I've applied to all areas of my life. The sheer size and complexity of the task or goal can induce anxiety and create a mental block that makes starting seem impossible. It's like staring up at a mountain you need to climb without any clear path or strategy for getting to the top. This sense of being overwhelmed can easily deter someone from even attempting to begin the task. The larger the task appears, the more daunting it becomes, leading to procrastination and avoidance.

Start by setting SMART goals. This is a powerful method to transform dreams into achievable targets.

SMART stands for:

- specific

- measurable

- achievable

- relevant

- time-bound

When creating goals, ensure they are specific by defining exactly what you want to accomplish. Make sure they are measurable so that progress can be tracked. Your goals should be achievable, within reach but still challenging. They also need to be relevant, aligning with your overall objectives. Lastly, make them time-bound by setting clear deadlines for completion. By following the SMART criteria, you can increase the likelihood of success in achieving your aspirations.

Furthermore, breaking down a big task into smaller, manageable steps is an effective way to overcome feelings of demotivation. Imagine, instead of one massive mountain to scale, you have a series of stepping stones that progressively lead you up. Each smaller step feels less intimidating and more within reach. This strategy simplifies the process, making the overall task appear more doable and less formidable. For instance, if you need to write a lengthy report, breaking it down into sections such as research, outlining, drafting, and revising can make the process feel more approachable.

Each smaller task should be specific and actionable. Rather than having "write a report" as your to-do item, you can split it into more tangible actions like "gather three sources on the main topic," "create an outline," or "write the introduction." Focusing on these bite-sized tasks reduces the feeling of being overwhelmed. This also makes it easier to get started because your brain perceives smaller tasks as less taxing, thus lowering the psychological hurdle to beginning.

Once you've divided your larger task into smaller steps, each completed step provides a sense of accomplishment. Completing a small task gives you a mental boost, which can help propel you forward to the next step. This positive reinforcement is crucial for maintaining momentum. It's similar to how a video game rewards you with points or achievements for completing levels; each small victory builds your confidence and motivation to keep going.

This sense of progress and achievement can be particularly beneficial for individuals with ADHD, who may struggle with motivation and sustained effort. Celebrating small wins creates a positive feedback loop that makes it easier to continue working on the task. It turns what was once a daunting mountain into a series of achievable milestones, each bringing you closer to your ultimate goal without overwhelming you along the way.

Key Takeaways

Having explored the intricacies of perfectionism and procrastination, it's clear that both play significant roles in hindering task initiation for individuals with ADHD. As you've read, setting unattainable standards can lead to a paralyzing fear of failure, while feeling overwhelmed by large tasks often results in inaction. Recognizing these patterns is the first step toward making meaningful progress.

Remember when we discussed the importance of accepting mistakes as part of the learning process? This concept is pivotal. Shifting your mindset from achieving perfection to valuing progress can dramatically reduce the pressure you put on yourself. It opens up a space where taking action becomes more important than doing everything flawlessly. Self-compassion is your ally here; being kind to yourself, especially when things don't go as planned, can make a world of difference.

Breaking down larger tasks into smaller, manageable steps is also essential. This strategy makes tasks seem less intimidating and provides numerous opportunities for small victories along the way. Each step you complete builds momentum, creating a positive cycle that encourages you to keep moving forward.

Procrastination often stems from a lack of motivation or interest in the task at hand. Finding ways to make a task more stimulating or enjoyable can be a game-changer. Whether it's pairing a dull task with music you love or setting specific goals and deadlines to create a sense of urgency, these little tweaks can significantly enhance focus and productivity.

Tracking progress over time is another effective strategy. By keeping a journal or using an app to log your achievements, you can visually see how far you've come. This practice not only boosts morale but also instills a sense of accomplishment. It's like charting your journey up a mountain, where each small step brings visible progress and fuels your determination to reach the summit.

Reflecting on past successes further reinforces this sense of capability. Keep a success log and revisit it whenever self-doubt creeps in. Celebrate your achievements, no matter how small they may seem. These reflections help build confidence and remind you of the strengths you already possess.

Setting short-term goals can make even the largest projects manageable. By breaking them down into smaller, actionable steps, you reduce the overwhelming nature of the task.

As you continue to understand and improve your task initiation skills, remember that progress is ongoing and non-linear. Embrace each step, celebrate your achievements, and be mindful of your growth. This journey is unique to you, and every effort counts. Start small, stay consistent, and watch as your abilities unfold over time.

In Chapter 4, we'll examine time management, another important aspect of living a happy and productive life with ADHD. Let's face it: Life can feel pretty chaotic thanks to our condition; however, with the right strategies in place, it's entirely possible to make everyday life more manageable and productive. Let's learn how!

Chapter 4:

Time Management

Managing your time and establishing routines is particularly challenging if you have ADHD. The whirlwind of daily tasks often feels overwhelming, leading to stress and disorganization. However, with the right strategies, you can get the hang of it! Whether it's breaking down tasks into smaller chunks, as discussed in the previous chapter, or using visual tools to stay on track, finding methods that work for you can significantly improve your ability to handle various responsibilities.

In this chapter, we'll explore practical techniques designed to help you better manage your time and establish effective routines. From the importance of planning your day and understanding time blindness to harnessing focus bursts and establishing good habits, this chapter will provide a comprehensive roadmap. You'll discover how to allocate your time wisely, use timers and alarms effectively, and create structured daily routines that foster stability and predictability. By implementing these strategies, you'll enhance your productivity and reduce stress, making it easier to navigate each day with confidence.

The Importance of Planning

Planning is essential for managing ADHD because it helps allocate specific time slots for tasks, reducing the feeling of being overwhelmed.

When you break down your day into manageable chunks, handling the numerous responsibilities that might otherwise pile up and become unmanageable becomes easier. For example, by setting aside a specific hour in the morning for responding to emails, you can avoid the pile-up of communication tasks that can feel daunting if left addressed all at once. This method makes the workload seem more feasible and gives you a clear structure on how to approach each day.

Moreover, planning assists in visualizing daily goals, which is crucial for enhancing task completion. Having a clear picture of what needs to be done makes you less likely to get sidetracked or forget important tasks. Visual tools like planners or digital apps can be extremely beneficial; they provide a tangible way to see your progress, which can be especially motivating. Knowing that after completing one task, you can move on to the next scheduled activity provides a sense of purpose and direction throughout the day.

In addition to helping visualize goals, planning allows for better prioritization, ensuring critical tasks are addressed first. I often struggle with determining which tasks are most important or urgent. By planning ahead, I can identify high-priority tasks and tackle them when my energy levels and focus are at their peak. This prevents the stress and anxiety that come from realizing I've neglected something important. For instance, if you have a big project due, planning out smaller, incremental steps leading up to the deadline can help you stay on track without last-minute panic.

A significant aspect of effective planning is that it provides structure, which minimizes the chaos that can often trigger ADHD symptoms. An unstructured day can lead to distraction, procrastination, and, ultimately, frustration when tasks remain undone. A well-thought-out plan acts as a road map, guiding you through your day and keeping distractions at bay. For example, dedicating certain times of the day to specific activities—work, exercise, leisure—can create a rhythm that makes it easier to maintain focus and productivity.

Planning also directly contributes to improving overall efficiency. When you allocate specific time slots for tasks, you're essentially creating a personal accountability system. This accountability can drive both productivity and satisfaction, as you will likely find that you accomplish more than you would have without a plan. Taking the time to review and adjust your plan regularly ensures that it remains effective and aligned with your goals.

Another key benefit is the impact planning has on long-term goal achievement. When you visualize daily goals, you're not just thinking about the present day but also how each task fits into a larger objective. This foresight can significantly improve task completion rates and keep you motivated as you see your efforts leading toward a meaningful outcome. It's much easier to stay committed to a plan when you understand how each small step builds upon the last to achieve something bigger.

Planning also reduces decision fatigue by allowing better prioritization—a common challenge for those with ADHD. Deciding what to do next can be paralyzing when multiple tasks vying for your attention. A pre-established plan eliminates this constant decision-making process, freeing up mental energy for actually doing the tasks rather than worrying about which to do first. Setting clear priorities in advance can guide you calmly through the day, making the entire experience more manageable and less stressful.

Lastly, the structure provided by planning helps mitigate chaos and disorganization, common triggers for ADHD symptoms. Consistent routines foster a sense of stability and predictability, which can be incredibly soothing. Knowing what comes next in your day can reduce anxiety and make transitions between tasks smoother. Whether it's using a physical planner, a digital calendar, or even a basic to-do list, having a structured approach can vastly improve your ability to manage the day effectively.

Understanding Time Blindness

Many people with ADHD have an inability to accurately sense the passage of time, a condition known as " time blindness." This often leads to difficulty in estimating how long tasks will take. For example, you might set aside an hour for a project that actually consumes three hours, disrupting your entire schedule.

This challenge in estimating time can cascade into more problems. Missing deadlines or frequently running late becomes commonplace, which can cause stress and anxiety. The result is that you often apologize for tardiness or feel frustrated about incomplete tasks. Constantly being late can strain your professional and personal relationships, fostering feelings of guilt and inadequacy.

Furthermore, the lack of time awareness plays a significant role in procrastination. With an unclear sense of how long a task might take, starting it is often delayed until the last minute, resulting in rushed, incomplete, or subpar work. The cycle of procrastination and last-minute rushing can erode self-esteem and create a perpetual sense of failing to meet expectations.

How to Combat Time Blindness

- **Set alarms and reminders:** Use alarms, reminders, and notifications to help you stay on track and be aware of time passing.

- **Create a visual schedule**: Use calendars, planners, or scheduling apps to visually map out your day and activities.

- **Break tasks into time blocks:** Divide your tasks into manageable time blocks with specific start and end times to stay focused.

- **Use time-tracking tools:** Explore time-tracking tools or apps to monitor how you spend your time throughout the day.

- **Establish routines:** Establish daily routines and habits to create a sense of structure and predictability.

- **Take regular breaks:** Incorporate short breaks between tasks to rest, re-energize, and maintain awareness of time.

- **Practice mindfulness:** Be present in the moment and practice mindfulness techniques to stay grounded and aware of the time passing.

- **Prioritize important tasks:** Identify and prioritize tasks based on their importance and deadlines to manage your time effectively.

- **Set time boundaries:** Set boundaries for your activities to allocate time appropriately and prevent time blindness from affecting your productivity.

- **Stay accountable:** Ask a friend, colleague, or accountability partner to check in on your progress and help you stay mindful of time.

By now, you should be noticing some recurring strategies. The great thing about managing ADHD is that mindfulness, for example, doesn't just help to improve your memory; it improves many other symptoms. Throughout this book, you'll see how one small action on your part will impact many areas of your life.

Using these tools consistently can build habits that mitigate the effects of time blindness. Over time, you can develop a more intuitive sense of time, even without the constant need for external reminders. This consistency helps establish a rhythm in daily routines, improving time management and reducing stress levels.

Harnessing Focus Bursts

Making use of short periods of intense concentration is a powerful tool for those with ADHD. Unlike the traditional approach of working for extended hours, focus bursts capitalize on the natural rhythms of attention and energy levels. These short, concentrated efforts can significantly boost productivity by providing a clear, manageable timeframe in which individuals can immerse themselves deeply in their work without feeling overwhelmed.

Scenario: Sarah, a college student with ADHD, is working on a research paper for her psychology class. She has been struggling to focus and organize her thoughts for days, feeling overwhelmed by the task. One afternoon, Sarah decides to sit at her desk and begin the research process.

As Sarah delves into the topic, she experiences a sudden surge of focus and clarity. She becomes fully immersed in reading academic articles, taking notes, and outlining her paper. During this focus burst, Sarah is completely engrossed in her work, effortlessly synthesizing information and generating ideas.

For the next two hours, Sarah is in a state of hyperfocus, where distractions fade into the background and her productivity soars. She feels a sense of flow, effortlessly moving through the research material and shaping her arguments with precision.

At the end of the focus burst, Sarah looks back at her progress and is amazed by how much she has accomplished in a short amount of time. With newfound motivation and a sense of achievement, Sarah is inspired to continue working on her paper, leveraging the momentum from her focus burst to propel her forward in completing the task.

In this example, Sarah's focus burst demonstrates the temporary yet powerful ability of individuals with ADHD to engage in intense concentration, unlock creativity, and make significant strides in their work within a concentrated period.

One effective method to utilize focus bursts is the Pomodoro Technique. We touched on this earlier in the book, but as a reminder, this technique involves working for a set period, typically 25 minutes, followed by a short break, usually five minutes. After completing four of these cycles, a longer break is taken. By breaking work into smaller, more manageable segments, the Pomodoro Technique helps reduce mental fatigue and maintains high levels of concentration. It also offers a structured way to tackle tasks, keeping distractions at bay and promoting a sense of accomplishment as each burst is completed.

Recognizing peak focus times is crucial for maximizing the benefits of focus bursts. Everyone has different times during the day when they are most alert and concentrated. Some might find their peak focus in the morning, while, like myself, you may be more productive in the afternoon or evening. Identifying these times allows you to schedule your most important tasks during these windows, ensuring that you're operating at your highest efficiency. By aligning tasks with your natural attention patterns, you can maximize your focus bursts and improve your overall productivity.

Incorporating focus into daily routines boosts productivity and provides a sense of control over one's time and tasks. Short, intensive work periods followed by breaks help maintain a balance between work and rest, preventing burnout. This balance is essential as it keeps you engaged and motivated without causing mental fatigue. Frequent breaks provide an opportunity to recharge, making it easier to return to tasks with renewed energy and focus.

Another advantage of using focus bursts is the consistent practice of task prioritization. Given the limited time in each burst, it's essential to identify and tackle the most important tasks first. This habit naturally cultivates better organizational skills and sharpens the ability to discern what needs immediate attention versus what can wait. Over time, prioritizing tasks becomes second nature, making it easier to navigate busy schedules and avoid the common pitfalls of procrastination.

The flexibility of focus bursts also means they can be adapted to suit various types of tasks. Whether you're working on a complex project that requires deep thinking or handling routine chores, focus bursts can fit seamlessly into any activity. We've established that breaking down a daunting task into smaller, more manageable chunks makes it less intimidating and more achievable. For example, instead of trying to clean the entire house in one go, divide it into sections and allocate a focus burst to each part. This strategy not only lightens the load but also keeps the motivation levels high as small, continuous achievements build up over time.

It's worth mentioning that tools and techniques like timers or apps can assist in managing focus bursts. Several digital tools are designed specifically to support those with ADHD, offering customizable timers, tracking progress, and even blocking distracting sites during work periods. These tools provide structure and accountability, making it easier to stick to focus bursts and maximize their benefits. With consistent practice, these bursts become a regular part of the routine, leading to sustained improvements in productivity and task management.

Establishing a Daily Routine and Good Habits

A structured daily routine is like a safety net if you have ADHD. It provides predictability, reducing the mental load of constant decision-making. When you know what comes next in your day, it's easier to stay focused. Think of it as creating a map for your daily journey; instead of feeling lost and anxious, you have clear directions to follow. Establishing consistent patterns can help reduce distractions and ensure you spend your time more effectively.

Part of your routine should be getting a good night's sleep. Maintaining a consistent sleep schedule is crucial for anyone, but especially for those with ADHD. Our brains and bodies thrive on regularity, and going to bed and waking up at the same time every day can significantly improve our mental clarity and focus. What's more, sleep plays a crucial role in managing symptoms and enhancing overall well-being for individuals with ADHD.

Benefits of a Sleep Routine

Quality sleep helps regulate your attention span and cognitive function. This makes paying attention and focusing on tasks the next day less challenging. When you get enough sleep, emotional regulation will be easier. More than that, it also reduces the impulsivity associated with ADHD, which will help you manage your emotions.

Sleep helps with information retention by aiding in memory consolidation, which leads to improved learning abilities.

A proper sleep pattern helps reduce the hyperactivity linked to ADHD.

Sleeping enough will keep your mood stable. This means fewer mood swings and irritability, which is a win-win for you and those around you.

Since executive functioning isn't what it should be when you have ADHD, getting sufficient rest can improve your planning, organization, and decision-making skills.

Overall, good quality sleep is essential for general well-being and mental health. It provides the necessary energy and resilience to manage your ADHD symptoms effectively.

Sleep is the foundation upon which everything rests; without it, even the best-laid plans can fall apart. Aim for 7–9 hours of good-quality sleep each night, and try to avoid screens for at least an hour before bed to help your mind wind down. Incorporating these strategies into daily life can significantly improve time management and overall well-being for individuals with ADHD.

Self-Care and Well-Being

I'm including a section on self-care in the chapter about time management because I want you to realize how important it is to make time for yourself. For adults with ADHD, the demands of everyday life can often feel like a mountain too high to climb. Constantly juggling tasks, responsibilities, and deadlines can lead to overwhelming feelings of burnout and stress. It's like trying to navigate a maze blindfolded, always feeling like you're one step behind. But what if there was a way to ease this burden and create a sense of balance in the chaos? Enter the concept of self-care.

I know it might feel like an indulgence, but in reality, it's a crucial part of managing ADHD symptoms. By prioritizing your own well-being, you give yourself the tools to navigate your daily challenges with greater ease. Think of self-care as the fuel that powers your engine; without it, you're bound to stall. When you carve out time for activities that recharge and rejuvenate you, whether it's a hobby, exercise, or simply a moment of relaxation, you're better equipped to handle life's myriad responsibilities.

What Is Self-Care for Adults With ADHD?

Self-care isn't just a fad or a passing trend—it's a crucial tool for those living with ADHD. At its core, self-care simply means taking intentional actions to care for your physical, mental, and emotional well-being. This can encompass a wide range of activities and practices that help manage symptoms and improve overall quality of life.

Practical Self-Care Strategies

- **Establish a routine:** Creating a daily routine can provide structure and predictability, which are key for individuals with ADHD. Set aside specific times for meals, work, relaxation, and sleep to help maintain a sense of order in your day.

- **Mindful meditation:** Engaging in mindfulness practices, such as meditation or deep breathing exercises, can help calm your racing mind and improve focus. Even a few minutes of mindfulness each day can make a significant difference.

- **Physical exercise:** Regular physical activity not only benefits your physical health but also has a positive impact on ADHD symptoms. Whether it's going for a walk, practicing yoga, or hitting the gym, find an exercise routine that works for you.

- **Healthy eating habits:** Fueling your body with nutritious foods can enhance cognitive function and mood stability. Focus on incorporating whole foods, fruits, vegetables, and lean proteins into your diet to support your brain health.

- **Quality sleep:** As you read above, adequate and restful sleep is crucial for managing ADHD symptoms. Establish a relaxing bedtime routine, create a comfortable sleep environment, and aim for consistent sleep and wake times each day.

Integrating Self-Care Into Daily Life

Self-care isn't just a one-time activity—it's a continuous practice that requires dedication and commitment. Integrating self-care strategies into your daily life can cultivate resilience, reduce stress, and improve your overall well-being. Remember, taking care of yourself isn't selfish; it's necessary for navigating the complexities of adult life with ADHD. Start small, be patient with yourself, and prioritize your mental and emotional health.

Incorporating self-care into your daily routine can nurture your overall well-being, optimize your mental health, and cultivate a supportive and empowering approach to managing ADHD challenges.

Key Takeaways

Throughout this chapter, we've delved into effective strategies for managing time and establishing routines to improve daily functioning when you have ADHD. We explored the importance of planning, understanding time blindness, harnessing focus bursts, and establishing a daily routine along with good habits.

Starting with planning, we saw how breaking down tasks into manageable chunks can provide structure and reduce feelings of overwhelm. By assigning specific hours for activities like responding to emails or working on projects, you create a roadmap for your day that helps maintain focus and productivity. This structured approach allows for better prioritization of tasks, ensuring that nothing critical is overlooked and that high-priority tasks are tackled first when energy levels are at their peak.

We then discussed time blindness, a common issue for those with ADHD. It's easy to underestimate how long tasks will take, leading to missed deadlines and heightened stress. Timers and alarms emerged as a practical solution, helping to keep track of time and reminding us of important tasks. When used consistently, these tools aid in developing a more intuitive sense of time, reducing the likelihood of procrastination and improving overall time management.

Harnessing focus bursts using techniques like the Pomodoro Technique offers another layer of support. By working intensively for short periods followed by breaks, you can maintain higher levels of concentration without feeling drained. Recognizing peak focus times and scheduling demanding tasks during these periods also maximizes efficiency and reduces stress.

Establishing a daily routine and building good habits were highlighted as essential steps. Routines bring predictability and stability, making the day less overwhelming and more manageable. Consistent sleep schedules and regular breaks contribute significantly to mental clarity and sustained focus. Small, gradual changes are key to embedding new positive habits without resistance.

The consequences of not finding effective time management and routine strategies can be far-reaching, impacting both personal and professional life. Yet, there's no one-size-fits-all solution. Each person must find and adapt methods that suit their unique needs.

As you move forward, consider the specific challenges you face with ADHD and experiment with these strategies. Stay patient and flexible in your approach. With time and perseverance, you'll discover the tools that work best for you, leading to improved daily functioning and a more balanced, fulfilling life. What new habits could you implement today to start seeing a positive change in your daily routine?

In Chapter 5, we'll examine routine in greater depth. We'll discuss why building habits and establishing routines are vital for functioning optimally as an adult with ADHD. Whether you struggle with maintaining routines or keeping your space clutter-free, this chapter will provide actionable insights and tips.

Chapter 5:

Organizational Skills

Developing organizational skills can be especially challenging for people with ADHD, but it is essential for managing daily life more effectively. These skills can help reduce feeling overwhelmed, as well as the disorder that often accompanies ADHD, making it easier to stay focused and productive. This chapter will explore practical strategies designed specifically for individuals with ADHD to help build better habits and maintain an organized environment.

We will dive into the importance of habit-building and how establishing routines can reduce decision fatigue. You'll learn about creating morning and evening routines that set the tone for a more structured day and improve overall well-being. Additionally, we'll cover the benefits of decluttering your physical spaces and offer step-by-step guidance on tackling clutter in a manageable way. By understanding and implementing these strategies, you'll be better equipped to create a balanced and organized lifestyle tailored to your unique needs.

Habit Building and Decluttering

Understanding the importance of building habits and decluttering can significantly aid in managing ADHD. Establishing and maintaining healthy habits is particularly crucial if you have ADHD for the following reasons:

- **Consistency and routine:** Habits create structure and routine, which are beneficial for managing ADHD symptoms and promoting a sense of stability.

- **Improved focus and attention:** Building habits can help improve focus and attention by reducing decision-making and cognitive overload.

- **Enhanced time management:** Habitual routines assist in time management and organization, making it easier to prioritize tasks and responsibilities.

- **Self-regulation and impulse control:** Habit formation supports self-regulation and impulse control, aiding in managing impulsive behaviors common in ADHD.

- **Task completion and productivity:** Consistent habits increase the likelihood of completing your tasks; they boost productivity and reduce procrastination.

- **Reduced stress and anxiety:** Establishing positive habits can lower stress levels and anxiety, giving daily life a sense of control and predictability.

- **Goal achievement:** Habitual practices contribute to goal achievement by reinforcing positive behaviors and progress toward long-term objectives.

- **Long-term change:** Building sustainable habits fosters long-term behavioral change, promoting personal growth and development over time.

By intentionally cultivating beneficial habits, you can create a supportive environment that enhances your well-being and ability to manage symptoms effectively and facilitates personal growth and success.

I know making decisions can sometimes feel overwhelming due to the many distractions and thoughts racing through our minds. Routines offer a structured way to navigate the day without constantly having to decide what to do next. When certain actions become second nature, it frees up mental energy to focus on other important tasks.

For instance, consider starting your day with a morning routine. By waking up at the same time every day, brushing your teeth, and preparing breakfast, you create a sequence of activities that require minimal thought. This predictability can be comforting and reduce anxiety about what comes next. Over time, these routines can lead to better time management and an overall sense of control over your day-to-day life. It's not about being rigid but creating a framework within which you can operate more efficiently.

Creating evening routines can be just as beneficial. Try to go to bed at the same time and use a few winding-down techniques to help you relax. Reading or meditating tells my brain it's time to prepare for sleep. By establishing consistent routines both in the morning and evening, you help regulate your body's internal clock, leading to improved mental clarity and emotional stability.

A Cluttered Space Equals a Cluttered Mind

Decluttering physical spaces is another essential aspect of managing ADHD. Living in a cluttered space can have a negative impact on individuals with ADHD.

Clutter can lead to sensory overload and increased distractions, which isn't what you want if you have ADHD. This will make it even more challenging for you to focus on tasks. What's more, a cluttered environment can easily contribute to disorganization and forgetfulness. The result? You'll find it difficult to remember important tasks or appointments.

Personally, cluttered spaces lead to major stress and anxiety, and this impacts my overall mood. I find it challenging to regulate my moods when I'm surrounded by chaos, and it's not uncommon for my ADHD symptoms to go into overdrive when facing excessive clutter. I also tend to feel overwhelmed easily, which leads to procrastination and, at its worst, avoidance of things I have to do. It goes without saying that this greatly reduces my productivity and efficiency.

I don't know about you, but for me, cluttered environments lack structure and routine, and this further complicates life with ADHD.

Scenario: Bob, a professional in his 30s, struggled with ADHD symptoms that often led to disorganization, distractibility, and difficulty focusing on tasks. His workspace and home environment were cluttered with papers, books, and miscellaneous items, creating a chaotic and overwhelming atmosphere that further impacted his ability to function effectively.

Recognizing the impact of clutter on his productivity and well-being, Bob decided to take proactive steps to declutter and organize his surroundings. He embarked on a decluttering journey, starting with his workspace, where he spent most of his day working.

Bob began by sorting through piles of papers, organizing documents into folders, and creating a system for categorizing and storing important materials. He cleared out unnecessary items, decluttered his desk, and set up a functional workspace that minimized distractions and optimized efficiency.

As Bob continued decluttering, he noticed a remarkable shift in his ability to focus and concentrate on tasks. With a clutter-free environment, he found it easier to locate important documents, prioritize tasks, and maintain a sense of order in his work routines.

The act of decluttering not only transformed Bob's physical space but also profoundly impacted his mental clarity and productivity. By removing visual distractions and creating a clean, organized environment, Bob could function better, reduce feelings of overwhelm and enhance his ability to manage his ADHD symptoms effectively.

With a decluttered space that supported his productivity and well-being, Bob experienced improved focus, increased motivation, and a greater sense of control over his work and daily life. By recognizing the connection between clutter and ADHD symptoms and taking steps to clear the chaos, Bob was able to unlock his full potential, thrive in his professional endeavors, and cultivate a sense of calm and clarity in his surroundings.

Creating an organized and decluttered living environment can reduce distractions, improve focus, and promote a sense of calm and control, ultimately enhancing their overall well-being and daily functioning.

How to Declutter

Start by tackling one area at a time, such as your desk or a particular room. Create designated spaces for essential items and ensure everything has a place. Removing unnecessary objects reduces the likelihood of being distracted and helps maintain a semblance of order. Investing in storage solutions like shelves and bins can make a significant difference. Remind yourself that this process doesn't have to happen overnight; it can be gradual, which makes it less overwhelming and more sustainable in the long run.

Regular maintenance is essential to keeping spaces decluttered. Set aside a few minutes each day to tidy up and put things back where they belong. Developing this habit can prevent clutter from accumulating again. When your living space remains organized, it naturally promotes a calmer, more focused state of mind. This ongoing effort helps cultivate an environment conducive to productivity and well-being.

Gradual habit formation will be particularly effective for you since large, abrupt changes can often feel daunting, leading to frustration and setbacks. Instead, focus on small, manageable changes that can be consistently practiced over time. This approach allows you to build momentum and create lasting habits without feeling overwhelmed.

Reinforcement is critical when forming new habits. As always, celebrate progress, no matter how small, as this will boost motivation and reinforce positive behaviors. Whether it's treating yourself to a favorite snack or simply acknowledging a job well done, these rewards provide encouragement to keep going. Habit trackers or journaling can also help monitor progress and identify areas for improvement. These tools offer tangible evidence of growth, further motivating you to stick with your new routines.

Consistent practice of these habits leads to better self-regulation and task management. As you become more accustomed to your routines and organizational strategies, you develop greater resilience against distractions and disruptions. This consistency cultivates discipline, making it easier to stay focused and complete tasks efficiently. The more you practice these habits, the more ingrained they become, eventually becoming automatic responses requiring less conscious effort.

For example, if you've established a routine of organizing your workspace every morning, it quickly becomes a seamless part of your day. You no longer need to think about doing it; it just happens. This repetition builds reliability and predictability in your daily life, creating a foundation for managing complex tasks and responsibilities.

Moreover, consistent practice helps improve your ability to prioritize and plan effectively. With a clear structure in place, you can allocate time and resources more efficiently, ensuring that important tasks are completed promptly. This proactive approach minimizes the risk of procrastination and last-minute rushes, leading to higher-quality outcomes and reduced stress.

Progress Not Perfection

When it comes to developing effective organizational skills tailored to the needs of individuals with ADHD, the focus should be on progress rather than perfection. Setting realistic expectations is crucial in this journey.

In Chapter 3, we discussed the trap of perfection, and you should apply what you learned there to all aspects of your life, including building habits.

Let's recap why setting realistic expectations and steering clear of perfectionism is crucial for individuals with ADHD:

- Realistic expectations alleviate the pressure to achieve perfection, reducing stress and anxiety levels.

- Setting achievable goals promotes a sense of accomplishment and boosts self-esteem, fostering a positive self-image.

- Realistic expectations allow you to focus on progress rather than perfection, increasing attention span and task engagement.

- Perfectionism can lead to procrastination and avoidance of tasks, while realistic expectations encourage action and task completion.

- Avoiding perfectionism supports emotional regulation by reducing feelings of frustration, disappointment, and self-criticism, which are common in ADHD.

- Realistic expectations promote flexibility and adaptability in managing daily challenges, providing room for adjustment and growth.

- Setting realistic goals fosters a sense of direction and purpose without setting unattainable standards, facilitating progress and achievement.

- Emphasizing the journey and effort invested in tasks rather than solely on the end result encourages perseverance and resilience.

By embracing realistic expectations and steering clear of perfectionism, you can cultivate a supportive and encouraging mindset, leading to improved well-being, enhanced productivity, and a greater sense of fulfillment in daily life.

As we discussed earlier (and you most likely know from personal experience), people with ADHD often set high standards for themselves, which can lead to frustration and burnout when those standards are not met. Setting attainable goals builds a sense of accomplishment and keeps moving forward. Recognize that it's okay to adjust your goals based on your circumstances and energy levels.

For instance, if organizing your entire home feels overwhelming, start with one room or even just one drawer. Breaking down tasks into manageable chunks makes them less daunting and more achievable. This approach reduces stress and helps maintain a steady pace without feeling overwhelmed. Progress, no matter how small, is something to celebrate because it's a step towards your ultimate goal. It's essential to remind yourself that everyone has their own pace and path to follow.

Also, when you complete a task or make progress, take a moment to feel good about it. In an earlier chapter, we discussed how important it is to celebrate even small victories. So, reward yourself with something enjoyable, like a short walk, a favorite treat, or some downtime with a hobby. These positive reinforcements will encourage you to keep going and make the process feel rewarding.

Another crucial aspect is understanding that setbacks are part of the process. Everyone faces challenges, and hitting a roadblock doesn't mean failure. It's essential to view these setbacks as opportunities to learn and grow. Instead of getting discouraged, analyze what went wrong and how you can adjust your approach moving forward. This adaptive mindset fosters resilience and keeps you from giving up when things don't go as planned. Remember, persistence is key to overcoming obstacles.

To illustrate, imagine you're working on improving your time management skills but find yourself frequently distracted. Rather than seeing this as a failure, look at it as feedback. Maybe your current environment has too many distractions, or perhaps your schedule needs adjustments. By identifying the issue, you can make necessary changes and continue your journey with better strategies in place. This process of learning and adapting builds strength and determination.

In the end, continuous improvement is more sustainable and rewarding than striving for unattainable perfection. Focusing on gradual progress allows you to build habits and skills over time without overwhelming yourself. It's about making consistent, small changes that accumulate into significant improvements. This approach is easier to maintain and leads to more substantial results in the long run. Patience and persistence are vital, as meaningful change doesn't happen overnight.

Creativity and ADHD

ADHD and creativity share a fascinating intersection that showcases the unique thought patterns and innovative potential of individuals with ADHD.

Embracing this connection can lead to boundless creativity and innovation. The divergent thinking that is part of ADHD gives you an edge. It helps you generate unique ideas, enables you to make unique connections, and promotes out-of-the-box thinking. This approach can spark innovative solutions and unconventional perspectives. We also tend to think disruptively and explore uncharted territories, which makes generating novel ideas and visionary concepts a common part of ADHD. The hyperfocus state we often fall into is another bonus for creativity, as it can lead to creative breakthroughs and unparalleled productivity.

When we look at the impulsivity and the willingness to take risks often associated with ADHD, we see another reason why we often explore new opportunities and don't shy away from experimenting with bold ideas. What is often thought of as negative symptoms helps us embrace uncertainty in the pursuit of our creative endeavors.

By embracing your unique thought patterns, unconventional approaches, and creative impulses, you can unlock your full creative potential, embrace your authenticity, and celebrate the richness of your imaginative landscapes.

By recognizing and embracing the inherent connection between ADHD and creativity, you can nurture your creative talents, leverage your unique perspectives, and contribute to a world enriched by innovation, originality, and the limitless possibilities of creative exploration.

Here's how you can enhance your creative side:

- **Embrace hyperfocus:** Leverage the tendency of hyperfocus to immerse yourself in creative activities. Set aside dedicated time to engage in creative pursuits without distractions, allowing your mind to focus intensely on the task at hand.

- **Experiment with different mediums:** Explore a variety of creative outlets, such as painting, drawing, writing, music, crafting, photography, or digital design. Trying different mediums can help you discover your creative passion and provide a diverse range of avenues for self-expression.

- **Set realistic goals:** Establish achievable goals and timelines to stay motivated and track progress while allowing flexibility for spontaneous bursts of creativity.

- **Create a stimulating environment:** Design a workspace that inspires your creativity and minimizes distractions. Incorporate elements like color, artwork, inspiring quotes, or music to enhance the creative atmosphere and foster a sense of flow during your creative process.

- **Utilize visual aids:** Visual aids such as vision boards, mind maps, sketches, or storyboards can help brainstorm ideas, organize thoughts, and visually represent creative concepts. Visual tools can stimulate creativity and provide a structured approach to creativity.

- **Collaborate and seek feedback:** Working with other creatives and participating in group projects will leave you with a fresh perspective and may inspire new ideas. More than that, the feedback you get may lead to improvement while you also foster a sense of community and support in the creative process.

- **Embrace imperfection:** Embrace imperfection and allow room for experimentation, mistakes, and revisions in the creative process. Recognize that creativity thrives on exploration, innovation, and embracing the unexpected rather than aiming for perfection.

By incorporating these strategies and approaches into your daily routine, you can harness and cultivate a fulfilling and expressive creative outlet that aligns with your strengths and passions.

Key Takeaways

In this chapter, we've navigated the world of habit-building and decluttering to create a more structured life that caters specifically to the needs of individuals with ADHD. We started by exploring how routines can serve as anchors in your day, helping you glide through tasks with minimal mental effort. You can find a sense of calm and control by creating predictable patterns, both in the morning and evening. This steady rhythm alleviates decision fatigue and contributes to better sleep and overall well-being.

We then shifted our focus to the physical space around you, emphasizing the importance of decluttering. A tidy environment promotes a tidy mind. By methodically organizing your surroundings, you reduce distractions and create a space that supports your focus and productivity. The process of decluttering doesn't have to be overwhelming. Tackling one small area at a time can make it manageable and even enjoyable. This step-by-step approach ensures that your effort leads to lasting change rather than temporary fixes.

Throughout these discussions, the overarching theme has been progress, not perfection. It's crucial to set realistic expectations and celebrate even the smallest victories. For someone with ADHD, setting high standards can lead to frustration and burnout. Each tiny step forward is a victory in itself and deserves recognition.

Moreover, maintaining a positive mindset is vital. Setbacks are part and parcel of any journey, especially one involving habit formation and organization. Instead of viewing them as failures, see them as opportunities to learn. Adjusting your approach based on what works and what doesn't will help you develop resilience and adaptability. Embrace each challenge as a stepping stone rather than an obstacle.

For example, don't get discouraged if you struggle with keeping a consistent bedtime routine. Analyze what might be disrupting your efforts. Is it the allure of late-night screen time or perhaps unresolved stress from the day? Identifying these factors allows you to tweak your routine and try again with a fresh perspective. This iterative process of trying, adjusting, and retrying builds strength and determination.

The ultimate goal is to create a sustainable lifestyle tailored to your needs. It's about making gradual changes that slowly but surely improve your organizational skills and overall quality of life. These small adjustments eventually accumulate into significant improvements. Patience and persisting through the ups and downs will lead to lasting results.

In essence, cultivating effective organizational skills when you have ADHD is a journey of self-discovery and continuous improvement. By focusing on making small, consistent changes, you allow yourself the grace to grow at your own pace. Remember, it's not about achieving a perfect system; it's about finding and sticking with what works best for you. Celebrate your progress, learn from your setbacks, and keep moving forward. As you build these habits, you'll find that managing ADHD becomes less about struggle and more about living a balanced, fulfilling life.

So, embrace the journey with all its twists and turns. Stay committed to making progress, no matter how small, and celebrate every step forward. With dedication and perseverance, you'll find that building effective organizational skills is possible and incredibly rewarding.

In the coming chapter, we're going to focus on improving impulse control—something that is particularly challenging for people with ADHD. We tend to act and then think about it later, right? Not managing your impulses can affect your personal relationships negatively but can also impact your professional standing when hasty decisions lead to regrettable outcomes. I think it's time for you to learn more about how impulse control issues manifest and how to manage them.

Chapter 6:

Impulse Control

It's not always easy to pause and think when you have ADHD, which can make everyday situations interesting, to say the least. We also tend to make choices leaning toward immediate gratification but with long-term negative consequences. Whether speaking out of turn during a conversation or making an impulsive purchase, these behaviors can create social and financial complications.

Throughout this chapter, we will explore various strategies and techniques aimed at enhancing impulse control for individuals with ADHD. From understanding the role of executive function and inhibition issues to practical steps like cognitive-behavioral strategies and mindfulness practices, the content provides comprehensive insights to help manage these challenges. You'll also learn about external controls, such as organizing environments to reduce temptations. Additionally, the chapter discusses the psychological mechanisms behind poor decision-making and offers tools to develop a consequence-based awareness. By implementing these methods, you'll be better equipped to anticipate impulsive actions and choose more thoughtful responses, ultimately improving your quality of life.

Inhibition and Regrettable Decisions

Living with ADHD often means grappling with spontaneous urges and impulses. I won't be surprised if you tell me that you struggle to inhibit your immediate desires, leading you to act before considering the broader consequences. This inability to pause and reflect can stem from challenges in executive function, making it harder for us to monitor our behavior and resist temptation. Understanding how inhibition issues translate into everyday life is essential to managing this aspect of ADHD.

Take, for instance, the difficulty refraining from interrupting during a conversation. For someone with ADHD, knowing it's polite to wait for their turn doesn't always translate into action. The urge to speak out overrides our internal brake system. This presents social awkwardness and can strain relationships as others might feel disrespected or overshadowed. Similarly, impulse control problems can manifest in financial decisions, such as making unplanned purchases and later regretting these expenses when they impact bills or savings goals.

Feelings of regret often follow these impulsive behaviors. Have you ever hastily replied to an email without thoroughly reading its content, only to realize the response was inappropriate or incorrect? I know I have—more than once! However, the immediate satisfaction of addressing the email quickly diminishes when one faces potential professional repercussions. Recognizing these patterns helps anyone with ADHD identify specific scenarios where impulsivity tends to lead to regrettable outcomes, offering a strategic advantage in anticipating and planning better reactions.

The real-life consequences of impulsive decisions can be deeply impactful. For example, impatience on the road can cause traffic violations or accidents, affecting not just your safety but also that of others. At work, blurting out ideas without fully forming them can be detrimental, as it may give the impression that you're not thoughtful or serious about your contributions.

Scenario: John, a 25-year-old individual with ADHD, often struggled with impulse control issues that had a significant impact on his personal and professional life. Despite his intelligence and creativity, John found himself in a challenging situation due to his impulsive behaviors.

One day, John received an email from his boss requesting a detailed report to be submitted by the end of the week. Instead of carefully planning his approach and allocating time for the task, John impulsively procrastinated and spent the day engaging in unrelated activities.

As the deadline approached, John realized he had not made any progress on the report. Feeling overwhelmed and anxious, he impulsively chose to submit a hastily written document that lacked depth and accuracy. His impulsive decision led to errors in the report and a lackluster presentation of the information.

Unfortunately, John's lack of impulse control also manifested in his personal life. During a social gathering with friends, he impulsively made an insensitive comment without considering the impact on others, leading to a strained relationship with a close friend.

The cumulative effects of John's impulse control challenges became evident as he faced consequences in both his professional and personal relationships. His impulsive decisions created misunderstandings, undermined his credibility, and caused setbacks in his career progression.

Reflecting on the situations that unfolded due to his impulse control issues, John recognized the need to address and manage his impulsive behaviors more effectively. By seeking support, implementing coping strategies, and practicing mindfulness techniques to regulate his impulses, John took proactive steps to regain control over his actions and make more thoughtful decisions in the future.

Through self-awareness, personal growth, and a commitment to improving his impulse control, John aimed to navigate challenges with greater resilience, enhance his relationships, and overcome obstacles that arose from his ADHD-related impulse control difficulties.

Impulsivity can also significantly damage relationships. Reacting sharply during disagreements without taking time to understand the other person's perspective can escalate conflicts unnecessarily. Over time, these patterns can erode trust and intimacy, potentially leading to long-term consequences like separation or estrangement. Thus, it's crucial to recognize and address these tendencies to foster healthier interactions and avoid unnecessary fallout.

That being said, you should also know when to give in to your impulses and act spontaneously. A friend of mine once reminded me not to take life too seriously, and he left me with a memory that always brings a smile to my face. Let me tell you about Alex:

Alex has ADHD and a knack for finding himself in hilariously awkward situations due to his lack of impulse control. One sunny afternoon, we decided to go for a stroll in the park. Alex's eyes lit up with excitement as we passed by a group of musicians playing lively tunes.

Without hesitation, he impulsively joined the musicians, picked up a tambourine, and started jamming along with sheer enthusiasm. As the melody picked up, Alex's moves became increasingly over-the-top, drawing the attention of everyone around us.

What started as a fun and spontaneous moment quickly became a comedic spectacle. Alex's lack of impulse control had transformed him into the center of attention, much to his surprise. His tambourine skills became the talk of the park, with onlookers cheering and applauding his impromptu performance.

Despite the initial awkwardness of the situation, Alex's infectious energy and genuine joy spread to those around him. Laughter filled the air, and even Alex couldn't contain his amusement at the unexpected turn of events. In the end, his lack of impulse control had inadvertently brought smiles to everyone's faces, turning a potentially embarrassing moment into a heartwarming memory we still laugh about to this day.

In the end, Alex taught me that sometimes, embracing spontaneity and letting go of control can lead to the most memorable and joyous experiences, even if they start with a tambourine and a burst of impulse!

Understanding ADHD and Decision-Making

Neurobiologically, people with ADHD often have differences in brain regions responsible for self-regulation, including the prefrontal cortex. These variations can lead to difficulties in delaying gratification and resisting impulsive urges. Moreover, ADHD often involves a deficiency in dopamine regulation, which impacts reward processing and can make instant gratification particularly appealing.

Cognitively, individuals with ADHD may also exhibit a preference for short-term rewards over long-term benefits. This tendency, known as "temporal discounting," can explain why you might prioritize immediate pleasures despite knowing the long-term disadvantages. Additionally, difficulties in working memory can impair your ability to hold information about future consequences at the forefront of your mind when making decisions.

Emotionally, impulsivity can be amplified by heightened sensitivity to stress or emotional triggers. When faced with anxiety or frustration, you might act impulsively as a way to quickly alleviate discomfort, even if the action later proves counterproductive. If you combine all these factors, it's easy to see why acting impulsively is so common when you have ADHD. However, identifying these psychological underpinnings empowers individuals to develop targeted strategies to mitigate impulsive actions.

What to Do

Several techniques can strengthen inhibitory control and minimize regrettable actions. Cognitive-behavioral strategies, for instance, can help reframe thought patterns and improve decision-making processes. By practicing mindfulness, individuals learn to become more aware of their impulses and create a mental pause before acting. This technique trains the brain to slow down and assess situations more calmly and rationally.

Another effective approach is setting up external controls or reminders. Alarms, apps, or sticky notes can serve as physical prompts to reconsider actions before proceeding. For example, placing a note on the credit card that says, "Do I need this?" can provide a momentary check against impulse purchases. Organizing your environment to reduce temptations, such as keeping fewer snacks at home to avoid impulsive eating, also supports better self-regulation.

Additionally, regularly reflecting on past impulsive actions and their outcomes helps reinforce the importance of inhibitory control. Writing down situations where impulsivity led to negative results and reviewing these entries before making decisions can strengthen resolve. Practicing this habit cultivates an ongoing mindfulness of the ripple effects of actions, gradually promoting more balanced and considered behavior.

Minimizing Distractions

Managing distractions is a Herculean task when you have ADHD. Environmental and digital distractions are two significant factors that can hijack your attention, making it difficult to focus on what truly matters. A cluttered environment brimming with external stimuli can make it hard to concentrate. Bright lights, loud noises, or even an unorganized workspace can compete for your attention, pulling you away from the task at hand. On the digital front, notifications from your phone or computer can be equally disruptive. Each ping or pop-up message is a lure, inviting you to abandon your work momentarily. Over time, these minor interruptions accumulate, resulting in lost productivity and heightened impulsiveness.

To combat this, one of the most effective strategies involves creating a distraction-free environment:

- Start by simplifying your physical space. Keep only the essentials on your desk and remove any items that do not serve your immediate purpose. This might mean storing excess stationery or moving unrelated projects to another room.

- Consider using noise-canceling headphones or white noise machines to drown out background sounds.

- Adjust your lighting to reduce glare and create a more soothing atmosphere that helps sustain focus.

- Utilize time-blocking techniques, set specific deadlines for tasks, and break down complex projects into manageable steps.

Effective time management can help structure your day, prioritize tasks, and reduce the likelihood of distractions.

- Prioritize tasks based on importance and urgency, and focus on one task at a time to prevent feeling overwhelmed and distracted. Setting clear priorities can guide your attention and help you stay on track.

- Consider working with a therapist, coach, or specialist trained in ADHD to develop personalized strategies for managing distractions, improving focus, and enhancing productivity. Professional guidance can provide valuable insights and support tailored to your individual needs.

By incorporating these tips and strategies into your daily routine, you can create effective barriers against distractions, improve focus, and enhance productivity in various aspects of your life. Consistent practice, self-awareness, and a proactive approach to managing distractions can empower individuals to navigate challenges and thrive in their endeavors.

Transitioning to the digital realm, taking control of your devices is crucial. Utilize settings to mute non-essential notifications during work hours. Many smartphones and computers have "Do Not Disturb" modes that can silence interruptions without blocking critical alerts. More advanced techniques include using applications specifically designed to block distracting websites or apps. These tools allow you to carve out focused periods of work, free of digital temptations.

I limit my screen time to two hours a day. This doesn't mean I only work two hours a day; rather, I am allowed to scroll social media, read blogs, and check non-work-related emails during that time. At times, I may even watch one episode of a series I'm currently following. I create an environment conducive to sustained attention and reduced impulsivity by making these adjustments.

Another vital strategy is the establishment of routines. We talked about the importance of routine on various occasions throughout the book. That is because it offers predictability, which can be incredibly beneficial for people with ADHD. Having a set schedule mitigates the likelihood of being thrown off course by unexpected events. Start by developing a daily plan that outlines specific times for different tasks, including breaks. Consistency in following this schedule helps train your brain to become accustomed to focusing on certain tasks at particular times.

In addition to environmental adjustments and routines, leveraging tools and applications can significantly minimize distractions. Numerous apps are tailored to help you stay focused. Some applications offer features like task lists, reminders, and timers, all designed to keep you on track. For example, apps like Focus@Will use specially designed music to enhance concentration, while others like RescueTime provide insights into how you spend your time online, helping you identify and eliminate distractions.

There are also tools designed to create a mental barrier against distractions. Browser extensions like StayFocusd or Freedom can block access to distracting websites for set periods, allowing you to dedicate uninterrupted time to important tasks. Similarly, productivity tools such as Trello or Asana can help you organize tasks and set priorities, making focusing on one thing at a time easier.

How to Pause and Consider Possible Outcomes

Developing the skill to pause and evaluate the consequence of your planned action is crucial for anyone, not just those with ADHD. Taking a moment to reflect on the outcome can significantly enhance decision-making processes. I know this can be especially challenging for someone with ADHD, as the urge to act immediately might feel overwhelming. However, with consistent practice and effective strategies, this skill can become a habitual part of your routine.

Taking a moment to pause offers considerable cognitive benefits:

- When you allow yourself a few seconds to think before reacting, you grant your brain the opportunity to process information more thoroughly. This brief period lets you weigh the pros and cons, consider alternative options, and anticipate potential outcomes. This can reduce impulsive behaviors and lead to better decisions, enhancing the quality of your personal and professional life.

- Pausing allows the mind to shift from an automatic response to a more deliberate one. This shift helps engage the prefrontal cortex, which is responsible for higher-order thinking and decision-making. By strengthening this neural pathway through consistent practice, you can improve your overall cognitive control and be less likely to make hasty decisions that you might later regret.

- Thinking before acting helps individuals with ADHD assess potential risks and benefits associated with their actions. Considering the long-term implications can prevent engaging in risky or harmful behaviors.

- Taking a moment to stop and think allows you to analyze the situation, identify possible solutions, and strategize effective ways to address challenges. This cognitive pause enhances problem-solving skills and promotes effective decision-making.

- Pausing before acting provides an opportunity to regulate emotions and manage reactions in a more composed manner. It allows those with ADHD to navigate intense emotions, respond thoughtfully, and avoid impulsive outbursts.

- Reflecting before acting helps align your actions with your goals, values, and priorities. By considering how your actions contribute to your overall objectives, you can make choices consistent with your long-term aspirations.

- Stopping and thinking before acting promotes self-awareness by encouraging you to reflect on your thoughts, feelings, and intentions. This introspective pause fosters a deeper understanding of one's behavior and motivations.

- Pausing to think before acting can enhance communication and relationships by promoting effective listening, understanding, and consideration of others' perspectives. It enables you to respond thoughtfully and empathetically in social interactions.

- By pausing to assess situations before acting, you can advocate for your needs, communicate boundaries, and make decisions that prioritize your well-being. This self-advocacy is essential for self-care and self-empowerment.

- Practicing the habit of stopping and thinking before acting strengthens self-control skills over time. Consistent mindfulness of one's actions and choices can lead to greater impulse control, autonomy, and self-discipline.

In summary, stopping and thinking before acting is valuable for individuals with ADHD as it promotes thoughtful decision-making, enhances impulse control, fosters emotional regulation, and empowers self-awareness and self-advocacy. By incorporating this intentional pause into your daily routines, you can navigate challenges, improve communication, and cultivate resilience in various aspects of your life.

Techniques to Act More Deliberate

Strategies such as mindfulness and CBT (cognitive behavioral therapy) can greatly assist in enhancing the ability to pause.

As you recall, mindfulness involves being present in the moment and aware of one's thoughts and feelings without immediate reaction.

Practices like deep breathing, meditation, or even simple, focused attention exercises can help cultivate mindfulness. Over time, these practices build mental resilience and promote a more reflective approach to decision-making.

We covered CBT in Chapter 1, but to refresh your memory, it is a type of psychotherapy that focuses on identifying and challenging negative thought patterns and behaviors. It's grounded in the belief that our thoughts, feelings, and behaviors are all interconnected, and by changing our distorted thinking, we'll be able to cope with life better.

CBT techniques also play a vital role in improving impulse control. Cognitive restructuring, for example, encourages individuals to identify irrational thoughts and replace them with more rational ones. This method helps break the cycle of impulsivity by promoting a thoughtful examination of potential actions and their consequences. Integrating these techniques into daily routines can create lasting improvements in impulse control.

Overall, CBT is a practical and evidence-based approach that empowers anyone to understand and modify their thought patterns, emotions, and behaviors to achieve positive and lasting changes in their mental health and well-being.

Another valuable strategy is role-playing scenarios to practice predicting possible outcomes. Role-playing involves simulating real-life situations in a controlled environment to explore various responses and outcomes. This exercise provides a safe space to experiment and learn. By repeatedly practicing different scenarios, you can develop a stronger ability to foresee the potential repercussions of your actions and choose more appropriate responses. Engaging in role-play scenarios can also help recognize patterns of impulsive behavior. By identifying triggers and typical reactions, you can gain insights into your thought processes and develop strategies to counteract impulsivity. These practice sessions can be done alone, with a friend, or under the guidance of a therapist and can be tailored to specific challenges faced by the person.

Feedback loops and self-reflection methods are essential in reinforcing the habit of pausing. A feedback loop involves regularly reviewing past actions and their outcomes to learn and adjust future behavior accordingly. Keeping a journal where you note instances of impulsive actions, the context, and the consequences can give you valuable insights over time. Reflecting on these entries can help understand the underlying causes and make conscious efforts to pause and evaluate outcomes in similar situations. Self-reflection can also involve setting specific goals related to impulse control and tracking progress toward these objectives.

Key Takeaways

Throughout this chapter, we've dived into strategies and techniques to improve impulse control. From understanding the root causes of impulsivity to exploring practical tips for minimizing distractions, we've covered a lot of ground. Remember when we talked about how inhibition issues translate into everyday life? Well, every tip here aims to tackle those very scenarios head-on.

Our current position is clear: improving impulse control isn't just about addressing immediate behavior; it's about creating long-term habits that foster better decision-making. We've looked at how impulsivity can affect finances, relationships, and even professional life. This isn't just trivial stuff—these areas shape our overall quality of life. When impulsive actions lead to regret or negative consequences, it's essential to have a toolbox of strategies to fall back on.

One thing to consider is the emotional toll impulsivity can take. Impulsive actions often lead to feelings of guilt, shame, or frustration, which can compound over time. Imagine repeatedly making decisions you later regret; it can feel like a never-ending cycle. Understanding these emotional triggers is crucial to breaking free and starting on a new path of mindful action.

Now, think about the broader impact. If more people with ADHD can manage their impulses effectively, the benefits spill over. Better financial decisions lead to less stress; thoughtful communication reduces conflicts in relationships; mindful actions contribute to safer driving and more productive work environments. The ripple effects are enormous and ultimately lead to healthier, happier lives.

So, as you move forward, keep practicing mindfulness and cognitive-behavioral strategies. Make your environment supportive with reminders and structured routines. Reflect regularly on your actions and their outcomes to strengthen your resolve. This journey towards better impulse control is ongoing but absolutely achievable.

Next, we'll explore the importance of flexible thinking and strategies designed to help people with ADHD navigate the complexities of daily life. We'll also examine confirmation bias and how it can trap people in rigid thought patterns. Let's get to it.

Chapter 7:

Flexible Thinking

Flexible thinking is a necessary skill for everyone, but it's especially crucial for individuals with ADHD. Life throws countless curveballs, and the ability to adapt can make a world of difference in managing stress and finding success. Those with ADHD often face unique challenges that can make flexible thinking even more vital. This chapter delves into what flexible thinking is all about and why it's so essential for people with ADHD.

In this chapter, you'll find practical tips on actively seeking out different viewpoints, questioning your assumptions, and engaging in reflective thinking. By understanding these techniques and incorporating them into your daily routine, you'll be better equipped to adapt and thrive, turning potential obstacles into opportunities for growth and personal development.

Understanding the Concept

Flexible thinking is a cognitive skill that involves adapting and adjusting your thoughts, perspectives, and problem-solving strategies in response to changing circumstances, new information, or unexpected challenges. Basically, it's your mind's ability to adapt to change. It encompasses the capacity to consider alternative viewpoints, generate creative solutions, and approach situations from different angles to achieve desired outcomes. Here are a few key aspects of flexible thinking:

- **Adaptability:** Flexible thinking entails being open to change and capable of adapting to new situations or environments. It involves embracing uncertainty, adjusting plans as needed, and navigating transitions with resilience and resourcefulness.

- **Creativity:** Creative thinking is integral to flexible thinking, as it encourages exploring innovative ideas, thinking outside the box, and generating unconventional solutions to complex problems. Creative thinking allows individuals to approach challenges from diverse perspectives and consider unique possibilities.

- **Problem-solving:** If you want to solve problems effectively, then flexible thinking is a must. It enables you to analyze issues from different angles, brainstorm multiple solutions, and evaluate alternatives to reach optimal outcomes.

- **Perspective-taking:** Flexible thinking involves considering multiple viewpoints. It requires stepping into someone else's shoes, appreciating varying opinions, and recognizing the complexity of situations beyond one's viewpoint.

- **Resilience:** Resilience is a key component of flexible thinking. It involves bouncing back from setbacks, adapting to changes, and overcoming obstacles with a positive attitude. Resilient individuals can navigate challenges with flexibility, persistence, and confidence in their ability to overcome adversity.

- **Decision-making:** Flexible thinking plays a crucial role in decision-making processes, enabling you to weigh options, assess risks, and consider consequences from multiple angles.

- **Synthesis of ideas:** Flexible thinking involves synthesizing diverse ideas, information, and perspectives to create innovative solutions or approaches. It requires integrating different concepts, drawing connections between disparate elements, and synthesizing complex data into coherent strategies.

- **Adaptive learning:** Flexible thinking promotes adaptive learning by fostering curiosity, exploration, and a growth mindset. It encourages you to embrace challenges, learn from failures, and continuously refine your skills and knowledge to adapt to evolving circumstances and opportunities.

Staying flexible in your thinking will enhance your problem-solving abilities, foster creativity, build resilience, and help you navigate complex situations with adaptability and agility. Flexible thinking empowered me to approach challenges with an open mind, embrace diverse perspectives, and discover innovative solutions that have helped me grow tremendously and achieve success in various aspects of life.

Let's look at some factors that may prevent you from developing your flexible thinking skills:

Confirmation Bias

Most people are guilty of choosing to believe information that corroborates their pre-existing beliefs. This is known as confirmation bias and often results in skewed perceptions, as people tend to overlook or dismiss information that contradicts their existing views. For example, if you believe you're not good at a particular task, you might selectively notice instances of failure while ignoring or downplaying any successes. This can create a self-reinforcing cycle where only certain types of information are acknowledged, leading to rigid thought patterns.

Confirmation bias can be particularly detrimental for individuals with ADHD for the following reasons:

- It limits you to a narrow viewpoint, preventing you from considering alternative perspectives and solutions.

- It can lead to impulsive decision-making and hasty conclusions without fully evaluating all available information.

- It inhibits effective problem-solving by reinforcing existing beliefs and inhibiting critical thinking, which is essential for individuals with ADHD.

- It hinders personal growth and limits opportunities for learning and development.

- It fuels anxiety and stress as you may overlook contradictory information, leading to uncertainty and cognitive dissonance.

- It can strain relationships as it may prevent you from understanding others' perspectives and fostering empathetic communication.

- By focusing solely on confirming existing beliefs, you may miss out on valuable insights, opportunities for growth, and new experiences.

- It can compromise problem-solving skills by inhibiting your ability to think flexibly and consider multiple angles when navigating challenges.

Due to our impulsivity and a desire for immediate validation, we're more prone to seeking information that quickly reinforces our beliefs. This can mean latching on to the first piece of supportive evidence we encounter without further investigation. Additionally, the impulsive nature associated with ADHD makes it easier to jump to conclusions and harder to take the time needed to evaluate all available information thoroughly.

The impact of confirmation bias on flexible thinking is significant. When people continuously reinforce their existing beliefs without considering alternative perspectives, their ability to adapt and change is hindered. This reinforcement of rigid thought patterns can make problem-solving and adapting to new situations even more challenging. It narrows our focus and limits creativity, making us less open to new ideas and solutions.

One way to combat confirmation bias is by actively seeking out opposing viewpoints. This means making a conscious effort to look for information and perspectives that challenge your existing beliefs. For instance, if you believe a certain approach to managing ADHD is the best, try researching alternative methods and consider their merits. Engaging with differing opinions can broaden your understanding and enhance your ability to think flexibly.

Another strategy is to question assumptions. Often, our beliefs are based on underlying assumptions that we may not even be aware of. By identifying and scrutinizing these assumptions, you can uncover potential biases and open yourself up to new ways of thinking. Asking yourself why you believe something and what evidence supports that belief can help in breaking down confirmation bias.

Reflective thinking also plays an essential role in combating confirmation bias. Reflecting on your thoughts and decisions allows you to evaluate whether you're falling into the trap of only acknowledging supportive evidence. This process involves pausing to consider different angles and implications before arriving at a conclusion. Reflective thinking encourages mindfulness and can help mitigate the impulsive tendencies associated with ADHD.

Ultimately, awareness is key. Simply being aware of confirmation bias and its effects can make a significant difference. Once you recognize this cognitive bias and understand how it operates, you can take active steps to counteract it. This awareness can lead to more balanced decision-making and improved mental flexibility.

By incorporating these strategies into daily life, you can work towards more flexible thinking patterns. Over time, you can develop the habit of questioning your own beliefs and opening yourself up to new possibilities. This not only helps overcome the challenges posed by ADHD but also fosters personal growth and adaptability.

Why Small Talk Is Boring

One reason small talk can be uninteresting for people with ADHD is that it often lacks deep engagement and emotional stimulation. I know I want to be part of a conversation that stimulates me mentally, and small talk seldom provides this. Remember, our brains are wired to continuously seek new and engaging information, so discussing mundane topics like the weather or weekend plans might feel painfully dull. Without a sense of deep connection or substantial content, it's no wonder that our interest can quickly wane.

Additionally, the predictability and routine nature of small talk can be another factor that leads to boredom for individuals with ADHD. Small talk tends to follow a predictable pattern: greetings, basic questions, non-committal answers, etc. This repetitive structure can cause disengagement because it doesn't provide the novelty or unpredictability that stimulates our minds. In these scenarios, what seems like a regular social interaction to most people can feel unbearably monotonous to someone with ADHD.

Considering all this, maintaining focus during small talk poses a significant challenge. I often find my mind wandering to more intriguing topics or getting distracted by my surroundings. This isn't due to a lack of interest in the person I'm talking to but rather an inherent difficulty in sustaining attention on topics that don't fully capture my interest. This causes my attention to jump from one thought to another, making it difficult to stay engaged in the conversation.

Some techniques can be beneficial for making small talk more engaging for individuals with ADHD. One strategy is steering the conversation towards subjects that both parties find interesting. Instead of sticking to traditional small talk topics, diving into areas of mutual interest can keep the conversation stimulating. Another helpful technique is asking open-ended questions, which invite more detailed and thoughtful responses, sparking a deeper dialogue. Open-ended questions break away from the predictable yes/no format and can lead to more engaging interactions.

Practicing active listening is another effective method. You can find nuggets of interest within the conversation to latch onto by truly focusing on what the other person says. Active listening involves hearing the words and understanding the emotions and intentions behind them, which can make any topic more engaging. It creates a dynamic exchange rather than a one-sided monologue, helping maintain your interest.

Flexible thinking can be a valuable tool for coping with small talk by fostering engaging and meaningful conversations. Here's how flexible thinking can help:

- Flexible thinking allows you to shift conversation topics effortlessly during small talk, keeping the interaction dynamic and engaging.

- Embracing flexible thinking promotes openness to new ideas and perspectives, encouraging you to explore various subjects during small talk.

- Flexible thinking enables you to offer creative and diverse responses, enhancing the flow of conversation and sparking interesting discussions.

- By employing flexible thinking, you can better navigate social cues and non-verbal communication during small talk, leading to more effective interactions.

- Flexible thinking supports empathy and active listening, allowing you to engage meaningfully with others' perspectives and experiences in small talk.

- Leveraging flexible thinking enhances problem-solving skills in navigating social interactions, enabling you to adapt to different conversation dynamics.

- Embracing flexible thinking can reduce social anxiety during small talk by promoting a confident and adaptable approach to engaging with others.

- Flexible thinking enhances communication skills, enabling those of us with ADHD to express ourselves effectively and connect with others through engaging small talk.

By utilizing flexible thinking techniques, you can overcome challenges related to small talk, foster meaningful connections, and enjoy social interactions with greater ease and confidence.

Why It's Hard to Switch From One Task to Another

People with ADHD often face significant challenges when it comes to task-switching. Task-switching requires cognitive flexibility, which involves the ability to move fluidly from one activity to another without losing track of the task at hand. Executive function deficits play a crucial role in this process.

This deficit in executive function can make even simple transitions difficult. For instance, moving from answering emails to starting a new project may feel like an enormous mental climb. Shifting gears can seem daunting once you're engaged in one type of mental activity. This isn't just about a lack of motivation or interest; it's a fundamental challenge rooted in how the brain manages tasks and priorities.

Moreover, when you finally switch tasks, there's often a residual lag. Your mind keeps drifting back to the previous task, making it hard to fully engage with the new one. This lag time can accumulate over the day, leading to frustration and reduced productivity. Hence, understanding that these challenges aren't a result of laziness but rather a structural issue in brain function can be a real game-changer for those living with ADHD and their families.

Emotional factors can also contribute to task-switching difficulties if you have ADHD. Emotional attachment to a specific task can make it hard to let go and move on to something else. Consider working on a project that you're passionate about. Shifting away from it to tackle a mundane chore can evoke feelings of reluctance or even resentment. This emotional tug-of-war creates resistance to switching tasks, increasing the time needed to complete them.

Interrupted tasks can also lead to feelings of frustration and anxiety. When you're in the zone and suddenly get interrupted, the abrupt shift can trigger emotional upheaval, making it challenging to smoothly transition to the next task. These emotions create a barrier that affects task-switching and can spill over into how well the new task is executed.

Furthermore, recurring interruptions can build a sense of apprehension. Each interruption adds to a growing pile of unfinished business, fostering a feeling of incompetence or inadequacy. This accumulated emotional baggage can become a self-perpetuating cycle, making each subsequent task switch increasingly more stressful and challenging. Recognizing and addressing these emotional triggers can provide some relief and enable smoother transitions.

Flexible thinking plays a vital role in helping those with ADHD smoothly transition from one task to another. Firstly, it makes it possible for you to adapt to change, which allows for a seamless transition to a new task without feeling overwhelmed. When you embrace flexible thinking, you can prioritize tasks based on your current needs and any looming deadlines, thus optimizing your time management during task switching.

Since flexible thinking improves problem-solving, it can help facilitate a smooth transition and reduce any possible stress. Being able to prioritize tasks effectively will also alleviate some of the anxiety associated with starting a task, sticking to it, and completing it.

In the end, with a flexible mindset, you'll be more productive as you'll be able to shift efficiently between tasks and maintain momentum as you go!

By incorporating flexible thinking techniques into your daily routine, you can easily navigate task-switching, stay organized, and optimize your productivity by seamlessly transitioning between different tasks and responsibilities.

Creating transition routines can also be highly effective. For example, stretching before starting a new task helps signal to the brain that it's time to change gears. This mini ritual acts as a mental bridge, making the transition feel more natural and less abrupt. Over time, my stretching routine has become a habit, significantly reducing the cognitive load involved in switching tasks. Give it a try and see if it works for you!

Key Takeaways

Throughout this chapter, we've delved into flexible thinking strategies that can help individuals with ADHD adapt and thrive. We've covered confirmation bias, the boredom of small talk, and the challenges of task-switching. Each aspect sheds light on the hurdles people with ADHD face daily and offers ways to navigate these obstacles.

Reflecting on confirmation bias, it's clear how powerful it can be in shaping our perceptions. By only paying attention to information that supports our pre-existing beliefs, we limit our ability to see different perspectives. This is especially problematic for those with ADHD, who might already struggle with impulsivity and hasty decision-making. The key takeaway is that being aware of confirmation bias and actively seeking out opposing viewpoints can foster more balanced thinking and improved adaptability.

In our exploration, we also touched on why small talk often feels unengaging for those with ADHD. It lacks the depth and novelty that they crave. This predictable nature of shallow conversations makes maintaining focus a significant challenge. Strategies like steering conversations towards mutual interests and practicing active listening can make interactions more stimulating and enjoyable.

Task-switching presents another layer of difficulty. The cognitive flexibility required to move smoothly from one task to another is often impaired in individuals with ADHD due to executive function deficits. Emotional factors like attachment to tasks and frustration from interruptions exacerbate these struggles. Techniques such as breaking tasks into smaller steps and creating transition routines can mitigate some of these challenges.

As we wrap up this chapter, it's crucial to recognize the broader implications of these flexible thinking strategies. Understanding these concepts can lead to greater empathy and better support for those with ADHD. On a larger scale, fostering environments that encourage flexible thinking could improve collaboration and innovation in various settings, from classrooms to workplaces.

While there are tools and strategies to assist, it's an evolving process of learning and adapting. Embracing this mindset not only helps overcome the challenges posed by ADHD but also paves the way for personal growth and resilience.

The last chapter of this book deals with emotional regulation. I don't have to tell you that managing emotions is particularly challenging if you have ADHD. But don't worry, in the coming chapter, you'll get all the strategies and techniques you need to manage your emotions more effectively—even on the days when you're spiraling out of control.

Chapter 8:

Emotional Regulation

Controlling emotions is hard for most people, but it's especially challenging for those with ADHD. Learning to regulate your emotions starts with cognitive-behavioral techniques, which involve reframing negative thoughts into positive ones to reduce emotional distress. That's only one of the tools we'll explore; we'll also emphasize the importance of developing problem-solving skills to prevent feeling overwhelmed and frustrated. Time management strategies are also highlighted to minimize stress and create a more organized routine.

Furthermore, the chapter explores the role of social support systems in emotional regulation for individuals with ADHD. I can attest that my friends and family have provided essential emotional assistance and understanding during very tough times, and hopefully, you have such a support network as well!

The chapter also introduces relaxation techniques such as mindfulness meditation, deep breathing exercises, and progressive muscle relaxation to help shift attention away from distressing thoughts and create a sense of immediate relief.

Emotional Regulation and ADHD

When you can manage and control your feelings in response to different situations, stimuli, and interactions, you successfully regulate your emotions. It involves recognizing emotions, understanding their impact, and effectively responding in a balanced manner. However, if you have ADHD, emotional regulation can be particularly challenging.

Since we tend to be highly impulsive, we tend to react before considering the consequences. This makes it exceedingly difficult to regulate and control our emotions. In addition to that, our hyperactivity often fuels our emotional response and intensifies our feelings.

Our inability to pay attention also makes it difficult to recognize our emotions, making it challenging to regulate and respond appropriately to cues and triggers. This can lead to stress and anxiety surrounding our emotional responses, which can exacerbate dysregulation, leading to heightened emotional responses.

Here are some further reasons why emotional regulation may be especially difficult for you since you have ADHD:

- You may have heightened sensory sensitivities, which can cause you to feel emotionally overwhelmed and react more strongly to sensory stimuli.

- The executive functioning deficit associated with ADHD can affect your ability to cope with and adapt to emotional situations.

- People with ADHD are also prone to rejection sensitivity, which makes the heightened emotional reactions to perceived rejection or criticism more likely.

- Social awkwardness and difficulties understanding social cues or norms may result in inappropriate emotional responses.

When you recognize the various factors that contribute to you feeling unregulated due to your ADHD, you can implement strategies such as mindfulness, cognitive-behavioral techniques, and emotional awareness exercises and effectively enhance your overall emotional well-being.

Coping Skills

Reframe Your Thinking

Cognitive-behavioral techniques are a powerful way to help people with ADHD manage emotions. One effective method is reframing negative thoughts into positive ones. This involves recognizing the negative thoughts that often lead to intense emotions and deliberately changing them to more positive or realistic ones. I think of CBT as confronting the bully inside my mind. For example, instead of thinking, "I always mess things up," I change it to, "I made a mistake this time, but I can learn from it and do better next time." By consistently practicing this shift in perspective, I experience less emotional distress and feel more empowered.

Scenario: Megan, a 30-year-old professional with ADHD, struggled with low self-esteem and negative self-perceptions that impacted her confidence, motivation, and overall well-being. Seeking to overcome these challenges, Megan embarked on a journey of self-improvement guided by cognitive-behavioral techniques, leading to transformative results in her life.

Megan worked with a cognitive-behavioral therapist to identify and challenge negative thought patterns that contributed to her low self-esteem. By recognizing self-critical beliefs and reframing them with positive affirmations, Megan gradually shifted her mindset towards self-compassion and self-acceptance.

Through cognitive-behavioral therapy, she learned to set realistic and achievable goals that aligned with her strengths and values. Breaking down larger goals into smaller, manageable steps helped her build confidence, track progress, and celebrate achievements along the way.

Megan acquired coping strategies to manage ADHD symptoms and improve self-regulation. Techniques such as mindfulness meditation, time management skills, and organizational tools empowered Megan to navigate daily challenges, reduce stress, and enhance her focus and productivity.

Cognitive-behavioral techniques also helped her enhance self-awareness by recognizing patterns of behavior, triggers for negative emotions, and areas for personal growth. Self-reflection and journaling gave Megan insights into her strengths, limitations, and opportunities for positive change.

Megan practiced cognitive restructuring to challenge and replace negative self-talk with more constructive and affirming statements. Megan fostered self-confidence, resilience, and a positive self-image by reframing self-limiting beliefs and cultivating a growth mindset.

She integrated self-care practices into her daily routine, including exercise, healthy eating, adequate sleep, and mindfulness activities. Prioritizing self-care enhanced Megan's well-being, energy levels, and mood, fostering a sense of balance and self-nurturance.

Finally, Megan engaged in supportive relationships and therapy groups to connect with peers facing similar challenges, share experiences, and receive encouragement. Building a strong social support network provided validation, empathy, and a sense of belonging bolstered Megan's self-esteem and confidence.

As Megan applied cognitive-behavioral techniques to her daily life, she experienced a profound transformation in her self-esteem, mindset, and overall quality of life. By envisioning a brighter future, embracing self-empowerment, and leveraging coping strategies to manage ADHD symptoms effectively, Megan embarked on a journey of personal growth, resilience, and self-discovery that empowered her to thrive and flourish in all aspects of her life.

Practicing CBT requires patience and consistency. To start, you need to become more aware of your thought patterns. Keep a journal where you write down negative thoughts as they occur. This helps identify recurring themes and triggers. Once these thoughts are identified, challenge their validity. Ask yourself if the thought is based on facts or assumptions. Replace negative thoughts with constructive ones that foster a more balanced outlook. Over time, this practice can lead to significant improvements in emotional regulation and overall mental health.

Moreover, incorporating CBT into routines can prevent emotional upheavals. Taking a few minutes each day to reflect and reframe thoughts sets a positive tone for the rest of the day. It's also helpful to use reminders such as notes or alarms to prompt reflection during stressful moments. The key is to create a habit where positive thinking becomes second nature. With persistence, these techniques can provide a reliable coping mechanism for managing emotions effectively.

Learn to Solve Problems

Developing problem-solving skills is another crucial aspect of emotional regulation. Having a clear approach to resolving issues when faced with stressful situations can help prevent feeling overwhelmed and frustrated.

Begin by defining the problem clearly. As always, break it down into manageable parts and identify possible solutions. Evaluate the pros and cons of each solution and decide on the best course of action. Implementing a structured process helps in tackling problems efficiently and reduces emotional turmoil.

It's essential to practice problem-solving in low-stress situations initially. Engage in exercises like puzzles or small projects that require strategic thinking. This builds confidence and hones the skill set needed for more significant challenges. Additionally, role-playing scenarios with a friend or counselor can provide practical experience and feedback. These simulations help in developing the quick-thinking abilities you need in real-life situations.

Seeking external perspectives also benefits problem-solving. Discussing issues with trusted friends or family can provide new insights and alternative approaches. Being open to feedback and considering different viewpoints can enhance one's ability to navigate complex problems. Over time, consistent practice and collaboration can lead to more effective emotional regulation and a greater sense of control over life's challenges.

Manage Your Time Efficiently

Implementing time management strategies is vital for preventing feeling overwhelmed, a common trigger for emotional dysregulation. Effective time management begins with setting clear priorities. Use tools like planners, calendars, or digital apps to organize and schedule these tasks. Allocating specific time slots for each task helps maintain focus and avoid the stress of last-minute rushes.

Also, avoid overloading your schedule with too many tasks. Understand your limits and give yourself ample time for breaks and relaxation. This prevents burnout and allows for better concentration on each task. Remember, quality over quantity leads to more satisfactory outcomes and less emotional strain. Regularly reviewing and adjusting your schedule ensures it remains manageable and aligned with your priorities.

I find that adding buffer times between tasks can be beneficial and removes a lot of stress when life happens. Unpredictable events can disrupt even the most well-planned schedules, but with buffer times planned in, you can accommodate such surprises without derailing your entire day. It also provides breathing space to transition smoothly from one task to another, reducing the likelihood of feeling rushed or overwhelmed. Together, these strategies can significantly improve emotional regulation by creating a more organized and less stressful daily routine.

Build a Support Network

Throughout the book, we touched on why you need to use social support systems. When it comes to emotional regulation, your friends, family, and support groups can provide essential emotional assistance and understanding when you feel frazzled. When you connect with others who share similar experiences, you walk away feeling validated and reassured. You feel less alone in the world when you can express feelings, share challenges, and receive encouragement. Knowing you're not alone in your struggles can foster a sense of belonging and reduce feelings of isolation.

Building strong relationships with empathetic individuals also provides immense comfort during tough times. Regular check-ins with supportive friends or family members create opportunities to discuss emotions openly. Sharing experiences and receiving feedback can offer new perspectives and solutions to emotional challenges. These interactions help build emotional resilience and promote a healthier coping mechanism for stress.

You shouldn't overlook professional support, such as therapy or counseling. A therapist specializing in ADHD can provide tailored strategies and techniques for emotional regulation. They can offer guidance on managing symptoms and navigating life's complexities with ADHD. I'm proof that engaging in therapeutic sessions regularly can lead to significant improvements in emotional well-being and overall life satisfaction. If I didn't have personal and professional support systems to carry me through the more challenging aspects of ADHD, I wouldn't be the person I am today, especially not someone confident enough to share what I learned throughout my journey to help others.

Relaxation Techniques

Meditation

One powerful technique for regulating emotions is mindfulness meditation. Mindfulness meditation encourages present-moment awareness, which can be a game-changer for those who struggle with attention and emotional control. By focusing on the here and now, mindfulness helps shift attention away from distressing thoughts about the past or future, thereby reducing stress and anxiety.

Starting with only a few minutes of mindfulness meditation each day can make a significant difference. You don't need any special equipment—just a quiet space where you can sit comfortably. Begin by focusing on your breath, noting the sensation of air entering and leaving your body. When your mind starts to wander, gently bring your focus back to your breathing. Over time, this practice can become a mental anchor that helps stabilize your emotions.

Consistency is key in mindfulness meditation. It's important to set aside a specific time each day for practice. Some people find using guided meditations available through various apps or online resources helpful. By making mindfulness meditation a regular part of your routine, you'll gradually build resilience against emotional turbulence, creating a stronger foundation for managing ADHD-related challenges.

Breath Work

Another effective technique for mitigating emotional distress is engaging in deep breathing exercises. Deep breathing triggers the body's relaxation response, which can counteract the physical symptoms of stress. When feeling overwhelmed, taking slow, deep breaths can help calm both the mind and the body, creating a sense of immediate relief.

To practice deep breathing, find a comfortable position and close your eyes. Inhale deeply through your nose, allowing your abdomen to expand as you fill your lungs with air. Hold the breath for a moment, then exhale slowly through your mouth, letting go of tension with each breath out.

Repeat this process several times until you feel a noticeable decrease in stress levels.

Deep breathing exercises can be done anywhere and at any time, making them versatile tools for managing emotional distress. Incorporate these exercises into your daily routine, such as during breaks at work or before bed, to maintain a steady state of calmness. Over time, deep breathing will become an automatic response to stressful situations, helping you regain control more quickly.

Relax Your Muscles

Progressive muscle relaxation (PMR) is another useful technique for reducing physical tension and anxiety. This method involves systematically tensing and then relaxing different muscle groups in the body. The goal is to learn how to recognize and release muscular tension, which often accompanies emotional stress.

To practice PMR, find a quiet place where you can sit or lie down comfortably. Begin with your toes, tensing the muscles tightly for a few seconds and then releasing them completely. Move up to your calves, thighs, abdomen, chest, arms, and finally, your face, repeating the tensing and relaxing process for each muscle group. Pay close attention to the sensation of relaxation that follows the tension.

By regularly practicing PMR, you can develop a heightened awareness of bodily tension and learn how to alleviate it more effectively. This technique can be particularly beneficial for people with ADHD, who may experience chronic muscle tightness due to ongoing stress. Incorporating PMR into your relaxation routine can lead to improved overall well-being and emotional balance.

Yoga and Tai Chi

Activities like yoga or tai chi can also promote mental and physical relaxation. These practices combine gentle movements, controlled breathing, and meditation, making them ideal for reducing stress and enhancing emotional regulation. Yoga and tai chi improve flexibility and strength and encourage a mindful connection between body and mind.

Yoga offers a variety of styles and poses, catering to all fitness levels and preferences. Whether you choose a vigorous flow or a gentle restorative session, yoga helps release physical tension while calming the mind. Attending a class or following along with online tutorials can provide structure and guidance, making it easier to integrate yoga into your routine.

Similarly, tai chi involves slow, deliberate movements paired with deep breathing. This ancient practice emphasizes balance, coordination, and mental focus, providing a holistic approach to relaxation. Like yoga, tai chi can be practiced alone or in a group setting, offering flexibility to suit your lifestyle. I suggest you find a group and practice with them. I've met many people who've grown to be great friends and valuable support at my yoga class!

Relationships and Communication

Considering that you may experience various relationship difficulties that stem from the unique challenges associated with ADHD, effective communication plays a pivotal role in shaping relationships. Before we discuss some ADHD-specific communication skills, let's look at how common ADHD quirks can lead to relationship struggles:

- ADHD can impact communication skills, leading to challenges in expressing thoughts coherently, maintaining focus during conversations, and listening attentively. This can result in misunderstandings, misinterpretations, and difficulty effectively conveying thoughts and emotions to others.

- People with ADHD may struggle with forgetfulness and disorganization, which can affect the ability to remember important dates, commitments, and tasks within relationships. This can lead to missed events, overlooked responsibilities, and feelings of unreliability from your partners or loved ones.

- Our impulsivity can manifest in relationship interactions, such as speaking without thinking, making quick decisions without considering consequences, or interrupting others during conversations. This can strain relationships and lead to conflicts or misunderstandings.

- While hyperfocus can be beneficial in certain contexts, it can also lead to neglect of responsibilities and decreased attention to interpersonal relationships. When you hyperfocus on specific tasks or interests, you may inadvertently ignore the needs and emotional cues of your partner or friends.

- Difficulties in time management and task prioritization due to ADHD symptoms can impact relationship dynamics. Procrastination, difficulty in planning activities, and inconsistent adherence to schedules can create stress and frustration within relationships.

- Emotional dysregulation can cause you to experience intense emotions and mood swings. Fluctuations in mood, impulsivity in emotional responses, and difficulty managing frustrations or rejections can strain relationships and lead to conflicts.

- Those of us who have ADHD may experience heightened sensitivity to perceived rejection or criticism. This can lead to emotional responses that can be challenging for our partners to navigate. Furthermore, misinterpreting social cues or feedback as negative can affect self-esteem and relationship satisfaction.

- Inattentiveness and distractibility associated with ADHD can make it challenging for individuals to focus on conversations, show interest in their partner's activities or needs, and engage fully in relationship interactions. This can be perceived as disinterest or lack of engagement by their partners.

To navigate the challenges posed by the condition, we require understanding, patience, and support from our partners or loved ones.

Clear communication, structure, and mutual respect are essential for building healthy and supportive relationships.

Overall, the relationship difficulties faced by people with ADHD stem from a combination of cognitive, emotional, and behavioral factors that impact our social interactions and emotional connections. By increasing awareness of these challenges and implementing strategies for effective communication, time management, and emotional regulation, we can work towards building and maintaining fulfilling relationships that are supportive and understanding of our unique needs.

Here's a closer look at the importance of communication for individuals with ADHD and how it can influence the quality of our relationships:

- **Clarity and transparency:** Clear and transparent communication is essential for effectively expressing your thoughts, feelings, and needs. Honest communication fosters mutual understanding, builds trust, and promotes open dialogue within relationships.

- **Active listening:** You need to be present when you're engaging in conversation, and that is why active listening is crucial. When you listen to truly understand the other's perspective, you'll be able to engage in the conversation attentively and show that you're empathetic to what they're saying. By actively listening, you can strengthen your communication skills and enhance relationships through meaningful interactions.

- **Navigating distractions:** Distractions can pose challenges to communication if you have ADHD, making it crucial to minimize interruptions, maintain eye contact, and employ active listening techniques to stay focused during conversations.

- **Managing impulsivity:** Impulsivity can impact communication by leading to spontaneous reactions or interruptions. Practicing mindfulness, taking pauses before responding, and actively listening can help you manage impulsivity and communicate more effectively in relationships.

- **Empathy and understanding:** Cultivating empathy and understanding in communication is vital for connecting emotionally with others, recognizing nonverbal cues, and navigating social interactions with sensitivity and compassion.

- **Conflict resolution:** Effective communication skills are essential for resolving conflicts and misunderstandings in relationships. Clear language, active listening, and collaborative problem-solving can help address conflicts constructively and strengthen relationships.

- **Expressing needs and boundaries:** Communicating personal needs, boundaries, and preferences is essential for establishing healthy relationships and maintaining mutual respect. Openly expressing boundaries and expectations can help prevent misunderstandings and foster harmony in relationships.

- **Support and understanding:** Building a supportive network of family, friends, and partners who understand and appreciate the communication styles and challenges associated with ADHD can provide you with a safe space to express yourself authentically and feel understood.

By prioritizing effective communication, actively listening, cultivating empathy, and proactively addressing challenges, you can navigate relationships with greater ease, foster meaningful connections, and cultivate understanding and harmony in your interactions.

Key Takeaways

This chapter has explored various strategies and techniques to help individuals with ADHD manage their emotions effectively. We began by discussing cognitive-behavioral techniques like reframing negative thoughts into positive ones. By deliberately changing our perspective, we can reduce emotional distress and feel more empowered in our daily lives. Keeping a journal to track thought patterns and using reminders to practice these techniques regularly can make a significant difference.

We also highlighted the importance of developing problem-solving skills. Breaking down problems into manageable parts and seeking external perspectives can prevent feelings of overwhelm and frustration. Starting with low-stress situations to build confidence and gradually applying these skills to more significant challenges can lead to better emotional regulation.

Time management is another critical aspect we covered. Setting clear priorities, breaking tasks into smaller steps, and using tools like planners or calendars can help reduce overwhelm. Incorporating buffer times between tasks can provide flexibility and prevent stress from unexpected events. By organizing our day effectively, we create a less stressful routine that supports better emotional balance.

In addition, we discussed the vital role of social support systems. Connecting with friends, family, or support groups offers emotional assistance and understanding. Sharing experiences and receiving feedback helps build emotional resilience. Professional support, such as therapy, provides tailored strategies for managing ADHD symptoms. A combination of personal and professional support creates a robust network that strengthens our emotional regulation efforts.

We also delved into relaxation techniques like mindfulness meditation, deep breathing exercises, and progressive muscle relaxation. These practices help manage stress and anxiety by promoting present-moment awareness and releasing physical tension. Whether it's starting with a few minutes of mindfulness meditation each day or incorporating deep breathing during stressful moments, these techniques offer practical ways to maintain calmness.

Engaging in activities like yoga or tai chi was mentioned as another means to promote mental and physical relaxation. These practices combine gentle movements with controlled breathing and meditation, reducing stress and enhancing emotional regulation. Yoga and tai chi improve flexibility and strength and encourage a mindful connection between body and mind.

As we wrap up this chapter, it's clear that managing emotions effectively requires a multi-faceted approach. Each technique we've discussed plays a crucial role in building a comprehensive strategy for emotional regulation. What's essential is finding what works best for you and incorporating these techniques into your daily routine. Remember, consistency and patience are key. It's okay to seek help and lean on your support system.

For some, the idea of implementing all these strategies might seem overwhelming. It's important to remember that change takes time, and small steps can lead to significant improvements. Start with one or two techniques that resonate with you and gradually build from there. The goal is to create sustainable habits that support your emotional well-being.

Adopting these strategies can lead to a more balanced and fulfilling life on a broader scale. You can navigate daily challenges with greater ease and confidence by managing emotions effectively. This improves your quality of life and positively impacts your relationships and overall mental health.

Conclusion

Reflecting on our journey through understanding ADHD in adulthood, we've touched upon numerous facets of this complex condition. If there's a thread that ties everything together, it's the realization that living with ADHD is not only about managing symptoms but embracing a holistic approach that fosters personal growth and self-compassion.

The first key takeaway from this book is acknowledging your diagnosis. It might sound straightforward, but many adults struggle to accept their ADHD. Denial can often lead to further complications, including increased anxiety and feelings of inadequacy. Acceptance is the first step toward taking control of your life. It's important to remind yourself that an ADHD diagnosis doesn't define you—it simply provides a framework that explains some of the challenges you face. Moreover, self-compassion plays a vital role in this process. Be kind to yourself and recognize that everyone has unique struggles. You're not alone, and there's nothing wrong with having ADHD; it's just part of who you are.

While having ADHD can present unique challenges, particularly in the realm of executive function, which encompasses essential skills like organization, time management, planning, and task prioritization, it is crucial to recognize that these challenges do not define one's potential for success. By implementing effective strategies and techniques outlined in the book, you can not only navigate these obstacles but also excel and thrive in your personal and professional pursuits.

I want to encourage you to adopt a growth mindset, viewing challenges as opportunities for growth and learning rather than insurmountable barriers. By reframing setbacks as stepping stones to progress and embracing a positive attitude towards self-improvement, you can cultivate resilience and perseverance in the face of executive function challenges.

You should also acknowledge the importance of outside support. Family, friends, and sometimes even professionals play pivotal roles in managing ADHD. Having people around you who understand what you're going through can make an enormous difference. They act as your pillars, providing emotional support and practical assistance. Don't hesitate to communicate openly with them about your needs and challenges. A simple conversation can go a long way in fostering understanding and cooperation. Consider joining a support group. Engaging with others who share similar experiences can offer invaluable solidarity and advice. These communities create a safe space to express yourself without fear of judgment. Hearing stories from others can often inspire new approaches and reaffirm that you're part of a larger, supportive network.

Professional help, such as counseling and medication, can also be incredibly beneficial. Therapists can provide strategies tailored to your specific needs, helping you develop coping mechanisms for various situations. While not a one-size-fits-all solution, medication can also offer significant relief from specific symptoms. The idea is to integrate these tools into your life so they work harmoniously with your personal goals and lifestyle.

Beyond professional assistance, there are everyday tools that can significantly enhance your productivity and quality of life. A calendar, for example, can be transformative. Whether it's a digital planner or a paper one, consistently keeping track of appointments, deadlines, and tasks can reduce the chaos ADHD often brings. Breaking down larger tasks into smaller, manageable steps and scheduling them can prevent feeling overwhelmed and increase your sense of accomplishment.

Another powerful tool is a journal for reflection. Regularly jotting down your thoughts, experiences, and feelings can help you gain insight into your behavior patterns. This practice aids in self-awareness and problem-solving. Over time, you'll start noticing triggers and developing more effective strategies for dealing with them.

Daily planners serve yet another purpose. They help structure your day-to-day activities, ensuring you stay on track with your responsibilities. Planning your day the night before can set a positive tone for the following morning, making you feel prepared and less anxious about what's ahead.

Another critical aspect is setting realistic goals. Celebrate small victories instead of focusing solely on long-term outcomes. These incremental achievements build momentum and boost your confidence. Remember, it's not about perfection but progress. Tracking these successes in your journal can be a fantastic way to visualize your growth over time.

Physical health is equally important. Regular exercise, a balanced diet, and sufficient sleep directly impact your cognitive functions and overall well-being. Physical activity, in particular, can be an excellent outlet for pent-up energy and stress, which are common among individuals with ADHD. Incorporating regular workouts into your routine can dramatically improve focus and mental clarity.

Additionally, mindfulness and relaxation techniques such as meditation and deep-breathing exercises can provide immense benefits. These practices help center your thoughts, reduce impulsivity, and manage stress. Finding moments of calm and stillness amidst the daily hustle can recalibrate your mind, giving you better control over your emotions and actions.

Ultimately, living with ADHD as an adult involves a multi-faceted approach. Accept your diagnosis and treat yourself with compassion. Above all, recognize that while ADHD presents its unique challenges, it's also an opportunity for profound personal discovery and growth. I want you to realize that ADHD is not a life sentence but a unique trait that can propel individuals to excel in various aspects of life when embraced and harnessed effectively.

By viewing ADHD as a source of creativity, innovation, and adaptability, you can leverage your hyperfocus, spontaneity, and out-of-the-box thinking to achieve remarkable outcomes. With self-awareness, tailored strategies, and a positive mindset, you can channel your energy toward pursuing passions, embracing challenges, and unleashing your full potential in personal, academic, and professional endeavors. By reframing ADHD as a distinctive attribute that contributes to resilience, ingenuity, and determination, you can transcend limitations, break barriers, and thrive in a world that values diversity, creativity, and individuality.

Armed with the insights and strategies discussed in this book, you're well-equipped to navigate your path with confidence and resilience. Remember, you're more than capable of leading a fulfilling, productive life with ADHD. Embrace it, and let your journey be one of continuous learning and self-improvement.

Thank You for Reading!

I hope you found *Why Can't I Get It Together?* (ADHD Edition) helpful
and enjoyable.

Your feedback is invaluable to me and helps others discover this book.

If you could take a moment to leave a review, I'd greatly appreciate it.

Scan the QR code below to leave your review:

Your support means the world to me. Thank you for helping spread the
word!

Warm regards,

Patty

References

Al-Saad, M.S.H., Al-Jabri, B. & Almarzouki, A.F. (2021). A review of working memory training in the management of Attention Deficit Hyperactivity Disorder. *Front Behav Neurosci*, 21;15:686873. https://www.ncbi.nlm.nih.gov/pmc/articles/PMC8334010/

Hoogman, M., et al. (2019). Brain imaging of the cortex in ADHD: A coordinated analysis of large-scale clinical and population-based samples. *Am J Psychiatry*, 1;176(7):531-542. https://www.ncbi.nlm.nih.gov/pmc/articles/PMC6879185/

Madore, K.P. & Wagner, A.D. (2019). *Multicosts of multitasking*. Cerebrum. https://www.ncbi.nlm.nih.gov/pmc/articles/PMC7075496/

Mandolesi, L., et al. (2018). Effects of physical exercise on cognitive functioning and wellbeing: Biological and psychological benefits. *Front Psychol*, 27;9:509. https://www.ncbi.nlm.nih.gov/pmc/articles/PMC5934999/

Mukherjee, P., et al. (2021). Neural basis of working memory in ADHD: Load versus complexity. *Neuroimage Clin*, 30:102662. https://pubmed.ncbi.nlm.nih.gov/34215140/#:~:text=Working%20memory%20%20%28WM%29%20deficits%20are%20key%20in%20attention,the%20prefrontal%20cortex%2C%20cerebellum%2C%20and%20caudate%20being%20implicated

The Pomodoro Technique. (n.d.). About Pomodoro. https://www.pomodorotechnique.com/what-is-the-pomodoro-technique.php

www.ingramcontent.com/pod-product-compliance
Lightning Source LLC
Chambersburg PA
CBHW061801120626
46550CB00005B/2081